MONEY MANAGEMENT

MONEY MANAGEMENT

Dollars and Sense for Christian Homemakers

Edith Flowers Kilgo

BAKER BOOK HOUSE

Grand Rapids, Michigan 49506

ISBN: 0-8010-5422-2

Printed in the United States of America

. . . a prudent wife is from the Lord.
(Prov. 19:14).

Contents

Women and Money

Do you know the recipe for a "stew" capable of destroying a marriage, precipitating a nervous breakdown, and enticing a Christian out of the will of God?

The "stew" is really quite simple. As a matter of fact, it has only one ingredient—money.

With divorce statistics rising yearly, experts have pinpointed three major factors as the leading causes of failed marriages—money, sex, and in-laws. However, of these three, money completely overshadows the other two. An estimated 70 percent of all divorces are caused by money problems.

Because of the importance money has on emotional, spiritual, and marital well-being, no Christian woman can afford to overlook the importance of learning to handle her money effectively. Yet many Christian women would rather not think about money, much less talk about it. To do so, in their opinion, denotes a lack of spirituality. After all, they reason, doesn't the Bible say the love of money is the root of all evil, and doesn't it also say that God will provide for the Christian's needs? Why then must the believer concern herself with money matters?

Repeatedly, the Bible emphasizes good stewardship. Basically, that's what good money management is. Management does not consist of greed or hoarding, but is good stewardship of that which the Lord has entrusted into your care.

Money itself is neither a good or bad thing. It is, in its simplest form, a means of conducting the business of our lives. Therefore, the more capably a Christian handles the money she has, the more ably she prepares herself for weightier responsibilities and leaves more time for other matters. The woman who manages her money well does not have to waste time on the telephone pleading with creditors, nor does she have to spend sleepless nights wondering how to cover all the incoming bills. It is only when the money starts doing the managing that trouble develops.

A great many Christian women have an unrealistic view of their role in the management of household finances. To many, playing ostrich is the only role with which they are familiar and they believe that by ignoring finances the problems will go away. Others, particularly women over fifty, may see the handling of money as unladylike and, with a shudder of disgust, pass the chore over to their husbands. But this attitude can lead to disaster if the woman finds herself suddenly without a husband to handle the money for her.

Other women, influenced by the erroneous and unscriptural views of other Christians, may consider the handling of money as sinful. For many, even the act of writing a check, is in their viewpoint, a serious infringement on their husband's rights as head of the household. While the Bible emphatically declares the husband's rightful place, it does not contain a list of what is to be defined as strictly masculine or feminine duties. Just as examples are given of men cooking (Abraham in Genesis 18:7-8, Gideon in Judges 6:19, Esau in Genesis 27:31), examples are given of women handling money (the virtuous woman in Proverbs 31:10-31, Lydia, the seller of purple in Acts 16:14, and the woman with the ten silver coins in Luke 15:8).

Many Christian women are sincere in believing that being the family bookkeeper causes them to usurp their husband's authority as head of the household. But does writing a check actually constitute money management or is it the carrying out of a necessary chore associated with money management?

One day as I was writing checks my telephone rang. When my friend Ellen asked what I was doing, I replied, "Paying bills." Ellen was horrified by my answer.

"You aren't supposed to do that!" she told me emphatically. "You ought to know perfectly well that the husband is the head of the household and money management is his responsibility, not yours."

I was stunned. I had handled the check writing for twelve years. Had I unknowingly been defying God's commands all that time?

Ellen continued to expound on her idea that women have no scriptural basis for involving themselves in family finances, and, as she went on, I found myself disagreeing with her. Finally, when she at last stopped for breath, I asked a question which had occurred to me during her spiel.

"Did your husband ever change a diaper or give a bottle to any of your children?" I asked.

"Of course he did. But what has that got to do with money management?"

"Nothing at all," I said. "It's just that it seems to me that if writing checks constitutes managing money, then perhaps changing a diaper constitutes raising a child singlehandedly."

"Of course not! Giving bottles and changing diapers are just chores involved in child raising."

"Well, wouldn't check writing be only one of the chores involved in money management?" I asked. "As I see it, check writing and bill paying are only mechanical aspects of money management. Real money management consists of decision making."

For a moment Ellen was silent and I was afraid I had offended her.

"Then who manages your money?" she asked finally.

"That's something Randal and I do together," I told her. "Both of us share in the decision making. I couldn't possibly imagine him buying a house or a car without talking it over with me. We have a budget to live with and it's one that both of us have agreed upon. When I write a check to the telephone company or the water department, I'm not managing the money. What I'm actually doing is implementing the money management plan we have already agreed upon. I suppose you could say I'm the family bookkeeper."

Apparently Ellen saw my point. The last I heard she was writing checks and balancing the bank statement and her husband was pleased to be relieved of a chore he despised.

While a great many husbands do unfairly dumpmoney responsibilities in their wives' laps, another great number of husbands take the opposite view that as the head of the household they have the first and last say in all money matters and thus dole out the wife's allowance as they see fit. While it is not my intention to contest any workable arrangement in any happy marriage, I do feel that Christian women who write checks and balance bank statements should stop feeling guilty about their tasks. As long as a woman does not become a monetary dictator, she has not transgressed any biblical laws when she writes checks and passes out the funds allotted for the running of the household. Proverbs 31:10-31 presents scriptural proof of this.

In these verses is a picture of the ideal woman—the one whom other women are called upon to imitate. And some of the most revealing verses about this woman show her as a competent money handler.

Verse 11 sets the scene: "The heart of her husband doth safely trust in her, so that he shall have no need of spoil." She is a woman in whom complete trust can be placed. Verse 16 shows her keen business sense: "She considereth a field, and buyeth it. . . ." Both the decision and the transaction seem to have been her responsibility. Verse 20 shows her sense of charity: "She stretcheth out her hand to the poor; yea, she reacheth forth her hands to the needy." It takes money to engage in benevolency. She apparently used her household money wisely in order to have sufficient left over to use in a charitable manner. Verse 24 shows her willingness to add to the family income: "She maketh fine linen, and selleth it; and delivereth girdles unto the merchant." She was conscientious enough to add her own abilities when the family income needed stretching.

The Book of Proverbs was written more than a thousand years before the birth of Christ, yet this chapter contains various references to the ideal woman's capable handling of finances. Perhaps the most significant point here is that the arrangement was apparently pleasing to both marriage partners. That is the secret of successful money management: a workable plan which takes into consideration the needs and wants of all members of the family.

2

Putting First Things First

Attitude Counts

How do you feel about money? Is it simply a necessary ingredient in your life or do you find yourself thinking about it excessively? Do you strive to live well on what you have or do you daydream of diamonds and yachts?

Attitude is the single most important factor in money management. How you feel about money will to a large extent govern whether or not you use it wisely. On the same income three separate families may achieve three distinct kinds of lifestyles. One family may live frugally, putting away every available cent for a future rainy day. The second family may live comfortably and be quite happy with their lifestyle. The third family may find it impossible to stay within their budgeted limits. The differences? Attitude.

Generally, when a woman ignores her budget and spends unwisely the real culprit is attitude. An expensive bottle of perfume is not just a good smelling liquid; it is an expression of the wearer's need to feel beautiful or wealthy or free of money worries. The woman who spends twenty dollars of her grocery money in this way is not really buying perfume. She is buying a temporary fulfillment of her fantasy. That is why it is unheard of for a woman to "splurge" on a case of canned soup or a fifty pound bag of potatoes. Those things don't fill the same need.

Christians in particular must develop a healthy attitude toward money. As soon as we develop a grabbing sort of greed, it is impossible to maintain a close relationship with God. Jesus said, "No man can serve two masters: for either he will hate the one, and love the other; or else he will hold to the one, and despise the other. Ye cannot serve God and mammon." (Matt. 6:24).

As long as the believer's attitude is such that she can see money simply as a necessary tool, her attitude toward God is unaffected. It is only when money becomes master instead of servant that trouble develops. Jesus said, "For where your treasure is, there will your heart be also" (Matt. 6:21).

A great many Christians try to solve their money problems by cutting expenses or taking on two jobs when the real solution lies, not so much in temporarily changing the financial picture, but in permanently changing the attitude toward money. In discussing the matter of food and clothing Jesus clearly showed that the solution is to put first things first. "But seek ye first the kingdom of God, and his righteousness; and all these things shall be added unto you" (Matt. 6:33).

The Christian who has her priorities in order can effectively cope with her money problems, because money problems are not usually caused by the lack of money but by the lack of proper perspective regarding it. It may be hard to believe, but millionaires sometimes get themselves into such a financial bind that they have to file for bankruptcy. If such a thing can happen to people who have more money than most of us will ever see in a lifetime, doesn't it seem that attitude, not amount, is the real problem?

Are Riches Sinful and Poverty Spiritual?

Have you noticed that evangelists and missionaries are frequently sent to the ghettoes and never sent to the exclusive areas of town? The cleaning woman and the garbage collector are readily ministered to, but the wealthy are often marked as unreachable. But nowhere in the Bible does God give any indication that being wealthy is of itself a sin. Abraham, David, Solomon, and Job were some of the greatest men in the Bible and all of them were exceedingly wealthy. Their riches didn't separate them from a desire to serve God.

An oft repeated verse is "For the love of money is the root of all evil: which while some coveted after, they have erred from the faith, and pierced themselves through with many sorrows" (I Tim. 6:10). Notice that this verse is directed specifically toward Christians. The love of money is a sin which can overtake believers as well as non-believers, or the poor as well as the wealthy. A destitute mother on welfare can be as guilty of loving money as a billionaire can. The amount of money a person possesses in no way determines his attitude toward it.

Perhaps a great deal of our reason for equating money with sinfulness lies in a misinterpretation of Matthew 19:24, "And again I say unto you, It is easier for a camel to go through the eye of a needle, than for a rich man to enter the kingdom of God." The "eye of a needle" was a small gate in the walls of Jerusalem. At night the main gates were shut and only by squeezing through the narrow "eye" could anyone enter the city after dark. Consequently, if a camel had to be taken into the city in this manner it was necessary to completely unload the animal to allow him to pass through the short door. The lesson in this story is not that rich people cannot be saved but rather that it is necessary for a person to put aside all encumbrances, including the love of money, when he comes to the Lord.

Lack of riches is not a measurement of anyone's relationship with God either. In recent years a number of potentially dangerous religious cults which stress poverty as the ticket to heaven have come into being. While the cult members pride themselves on being poor, they are falling into the same trap of wrong thinking into which many rich people fall. Just as the presence of a great deal of money does not assure damnation, neither does the absence of money assure salvation. The twelve disciples did live simply and economically, but remember Judas was also a member of the group. Lack of earthly goods certainly didn't give him piety.

Any Christian woman who genuinely desires to serve the Lord through good stewardship of the money He has allotted to her, will find it necessary to settle the matter of money and its effects on spirituality in her own mind.

The Difference Between Wants and Needs

It is a rare mother who at one time or another hasn't been approached by a child with an outstretched hand and a pleading voice: "Mother, can I have some money? I *need* an ice cream cone!" We chuckle over a child's confusion over the difference between needs and wants, but when an adult has that same kind of confusion, the matter is serious.

For the woman who is having difficulties stretching her household budget, learning to differentiate between wants and needs is vital. Yes, we need food, but it doesn't have to be steaks and roasts. Certainly we need adequate clothing, but it doesn't have to wear a designer's label. Of course we need a home, but obtaining one should not necessitate the husband's having to work two jobs.

God recognizes our real needs and attends to them as we depend on Him. In his exhortation on money and goods and spiritual commitment, Jesus mentioned *needs* (Matt. 6:31). Philippians 4:19 says, "But my God shall supply all your need according to his riches in glory by Christ Jesus."

Money and Stewardship

The way a woman handles her money is one of the surest measurements of the character she possesses.

Certainly the woman who has committed her finances to the Lord will use a portion of them for Him, but that alone is not the only indication of her total spiritual commitment. Thousands of Christians tithe regularly and even give sacrificially, yet do not understand the principle involved in good stewardship of the money they have.

Good stewardship involves giving to the Lord, but it is much, much more than that. Stewardship is using anything you possess in a manner pleasing to God. The little boy with the loaves and fishes exercised good stewardship as did the woman who put her last two mites into the collection plate. Stewardship is not daydreaming of all the wonderful "good works" you could do with a million dollars. Instead, stewardship consists of using what you have right now, whether it be loaves and fishes or small change.

Money represents the most tangible and visible asset the Christian has with which to exercise stewardship and to use as a means of Christian witness. Your neighbor might never know you give regularly to missions but she can't help noticing when the two of you go shopping that your twenty dollar bill goes further than hers. Likewise, when her marriage is coming apart because of money worries she can see the difference your stewardship has made in your marriage.

Good money management presents to the world a picture of a person who has been changed. What better way can you show Christ's example in your life than by witnessing for Him in the management of your money? Those who might never sit still long enough to hear you tell of Him can see Him in your life if you are the kind of steward He wants you to be.

The real witness you present for Christ is what you are. A wise saying goes, "What you are speaks so loudly I can't hear what you are saying." The Christian who exercises good stewardship of her money is speaking loudly to a world which doesn't believe Christianity works on the practical level. The Christian woman who can live within her means and can present a serene face to a world in the grip of inflation and greed has gone a long way in showing her neighbor that Christianity is not just a religion but a committed way of life.

It is imperative that the believer who would show Christ to the world do so consistently in every aspect of his life. Yet money is usually the last thing people are willing to relinquish to God. Matthew 19:16-22 illustrates this point.

One day a wealthy young man came to see Jesus. Apparently the young man was sincere in his desire to do the right thing because he had already studied God's Word and was making an attempt to obey the commandments. Jesus went immediately to the heart of the young man's problem: he needed to be a good steward of the riches God had given him. Jesus required of the man the one thing that he was unwilling to commit to the Lord—his money.

A church treasurer once told me that money is one of the most accurate measurements he knows for determining any Christian's spiritual commitment. During ten years of service he had the opportunity to observe a great deal of giving. Without fail, those who sank themselves into debt let their financial commitment to the church slide first. After their money was no longer committed it became easier and easier to skip services. As far as that church treasurer is concerned, good stewardship of finances reflects on any Christian's commitment to all aspects of his spiritual life.

Discussing the matter of stewardship of money, Jesus told his disciples, "He that is faithful in that which is least is faithful also in much: and he that is unjust in the least is unjust also in much" (Luke 16:10). To further make the point of the correlation between good stewardship of earthly goods and the acquiring of heavenly rewards, He added, "If therefore ye have not been faithful in the unrighteous mammon, who will commit to your trust the true riches?" (Luke 16:11).

God's Portion First

"Money, money, money!" grumbled a tight-fisted church member one day. "You preachers want to talk about giving all the time!"

"Maybe that's true," his pastor agreed, "but if everybody would just *do* it we could stop talking about it!"

Giving to God is one of the most important aspects of a Christian woman's good stewardship of her money. The importance of giving to God can hardly be ignored when the subject is mentioned in the Bible 1520 times.

Giving God His tenth of her income is the Christian woman's first step in keeping herself on the right financial track. The tenth is not an offering. It is the *least* that is expected of us. Not only that, it is to be the *first* thing we deduct from our income. As far back as Abraham's day, the tithe was expected. Even 1500 years before Christ was born God was commanding the Israelites to give. "...of that wherewith the Lord thy God hath blessed thee thou shalt give unto him" (Deut. 15:14).

But sometimes the tithe can be a perplexing problem for women. What is a woman to do if she knows that good stewardship demands a tithe, but her husband, who is not a Christian, does not go along with her beliefs? Should she tithe anyway and risk causing friction and possibly alienating him even further from serving Christ? Each wife who is faced with this problem will need to examine her own situation and to pray about her actions.

A few years ago the wife of a non-tithing Christian told me how she handled this dilemma. The couple was in their mid-fifties and the family finances were handled in a rather conservative traditional manner. The husband had sole responsibility over each expenditure, and the wife had never even written a check. Each week, however the husband gave her what he called "the housekeeping money." Out of this sum she was to buy the groceries and cleaning supplies and have a modest allowance left over to spend as she chose. The husband left the entire decision of the handling of this sum to his wife. She began a practice of tithing 10 percent of her household money. It was not the solution she had hoped for, but she felt that God would hold her responsible for only that portion of the income over which she personally exercised control.

Of course, if the wife works outside the home, the problem is a bit different. Most working wives do control their own paychecks to a great extent, and many with unsaved husbands have resolved their tithing dilemmas by giving 10 percent of their salaries without making any demands on their husbands' salaries.

What Happens When Christians Give?

A friend of mine is fond of telling a story about a little boy who went shopping with his mother. The storekeeper noticed the child and offered him a handful of candy. Holding a jar of candy in front of the boy, the storekeeper told him to reach in and get a handful. Bashfully, the boy stuck his hands behind his back, stared at the floor, and shook his head. Again the storekeeper urged him to reach in and get the candy. Finally, when the boy refused for the third time, the storekeeper reached his own hand in and scooped out the candy. Eagerly, the boy then held out both of his small hands and received the gift. As they left the store the mother scolded her son for his refusal to take the candy when it was first offered to him.

"Why didn't you just put your hand in that jar and get the candy?" she demanded.

Contentedly the boy munched his candy and then looked slyly at his mother. "Because his hand is bigger than mine. If I'd gotten the candy for myself I wouldn't have gotten half as much!"

Christians, too, have frequently discovered the value in letting God do the scooping. After all, His hand is bigger than ours and the scoops He provides are much more generous than those we can get for ourselves.

Some Christians are embarrassed to discuss the fact of giving tithes and offerings in the hope of being blessed by their giving. However, the subject doesn't embarrass God at all. As a matter of fact, He not only says that giving to Him is the source of blessing, He offers the Christian a challenge to prove it.

> Bring ye all the tithes into the storehouse, that there may be meat in mine house, and prove me now herewith, saith the Lord of hosts, if I will not open you the windows of heaven, and pour you out a blessing, that there shall not be room enough to receive it (Mal. 3:10).

As one Christian put it, "It doesn't matter how much or how fast I shovel out to God; He just uses a bigger shovel and shovels more right back to me!"

Giving is the first step of faith in depending on God to supply your material needs. What you give to Him is in part what He uses as the measurement of what He gives to you. Remember the parable of the three stewards who were given talents. The one who hid his in the ground gained no blessing from it, but those two who put the money to work were commended by their master.

Sometimes when believers get into serious financial troubles their first thought is to take their tithes and offerings and apply this money to their outstanding debts. While it is certainly true that the Lord expects Christians to pay their financial responsibilities, robbing Him of His money is not the way to accomplish this goal. Your gift to Him is the seed by which the blessings from Him grow. Consequently, if you don't plant that seed, you can scarcely expect to have a harvest of blessings. "Give, and it shall be given unto you; good measure, pressed down, and shaken together, and running over, shall men give into your bosom. For with the same measure that ye mete withal it shall be measured to you again" (Luke 6:38).

Creating a Workable Budget

A Bag Full of Holes

Budget is derived from a Latin word meaning "bag." A bag holds things and keeps them from being spilled or misplaced. A budget can do that for your finances, too. When you put your spending in the form of a bag you will know precisely where your money is and will see that the putting into the bag and the taking out of the bag must work in harmony.

Developing a workable budget is the only way to control your spending rather than letting it control you. The budget that suffocates you or takes over and runs you is not the right kind of bag. The budget that is too loosely woven won't work either. A bag full of holes lets all your money get away from you and the result is that in spite of an adequate income you cannot make ends meet:

> "Ye have sown much, and bring in little; ye eat, but ye have not enough; ye drink, but ye are not filled with drink; ye clothe you, but there is none warm; and he that earneth wages earneth wages to put it into a bag with holes" (Hag. 1:6).

Start at the Beginning

Before you put pencil to paper to itemize the elements of your proposed budget, stop and think about your relationship to the money you have to spend. In Chapter One, we discussed attitude and its importance on your money management decisions. Now, as you begin to plan a budget, attitude gains new importance. That is why, given two families of equal size and equal income, no one budget will fit both. Any budget that is going to work must take into account more than dollars and cents.

From the psychological viewpoint money is much more than a medium of exchange. Our management of it says a great deal about our feelings for our family and our self. To some people money represents personal worth, happiness, and success. (Of course, the Christian has the responsibility of ridding herself of these erroneous views.) To other people money is almost superfluous.It is all right with them if they have it and it is equally all right if they don't. This kind of attitude can also be disastrous to budget planning. To still other people *now* is the important time and they will worry about college expense or old age when and if the occasion arises. To people like this, long-range planning seems a waste of time.

Try to visualize the things that are important to you. Are you unconcerned about the model of car you drive but insist on being well-dressed? Is a home of your own essential to you or are you content to live in an apartment and forego maintenance chores and yard work? Do you have your children in a Christian school even though doing so means eating meatless meals occasionally?

All of these things are important factors in your budget decisions. You cannot live your life in accordance with another person's goals, and for that reason any budget you devise *must* take your personal preferences into account. Just because I don't care what make or model year my car is as long as it gets me where I want to go, doesn't mean your feelings will be the same. Just because my family enjoys free entertainment such as museums, parks, and libraries in order to save money for putting my daughter in a Christian school, does not give me the right to tell you to do the same. For some people a good, late model car is a necessity. For others, a weekly ball game or a new record is important as a means of relaxation. It all depends on you.

Nothing you really care about should be eliminated from your budget simply because someone else may see it as frivolous or unnecessary. The object is not to deprive yourself of all the pleasure of spending your money but rather to give you an opportunity to have more of it to spend. If spending fifteen dollars a week at the beauty shop makes you happy, then by all means continue to do it if you can do so by eliminating some other fifteen-dollar expenditure which you don't care about quite as much. However, whether you studied the new math or the old, it is evident that you can only add new expenses to the budget by eliminating some old expenses or by increasing the amount of money with which you are working.

Where Do I Start?

The obvious place to start is with income. Write down all sources of income you have each month. Don't include variables such as possible cash birthday gifts or hoped for overtime. Write down only what you know you can reasonably expect to have to work with. If your job involves a variable income derived from such things as tips or commissions, try to arrive at a reasonable estimate of an average amount.

Don't forget to include any interest you might be receiving on savings accounts. If you are expecting a check as a tax refund, that amount can be included also. The important thing is to know how much you have.

Often the tally of income will be discouraging. Even before adding up the expenses you may see that the amount coming in is not enough, and you may be tempted to throw the budget plan away in despair. But that would be a great mistake, because as Christians we are not limited to figures listed in black and white. God has a way of providing extra income for those who are honoring Him with their tithes and offerings and who are struggling to handle their money in conscientious ways.

Remember the time when tax money was needed by the disciples and the Lord arranged for them to obtain it from the mouth of a fish? (Matt. 17:24-27). How about the widow who aided Elijah and then discovered she had a miracle in her grocery pantry? Although originally she had only enough for one meal, as long as she did what the Lord required of her, her barrel of meal and cruse of oil did not give out (I Kings 17:8-16).

What About Expenditures?

The second part of making a budget consists of listing those things which must be paid. For the Christian, this list is headed by the 10 percent tithe which belongs to the Lord. Then comes such things as mortgage payments, utility bills, etc.

After all the "must" bills are listed, add up the total and subtract it from your anticipated monthly income figure. The amount left will tell you just what you have left to divide among such things as groceries, gasoline, lunch money and allowances, gift giving, and clothing expenditures.

If you are already having financial problems it is quite likely that what will be left after the bills are paid is not going to be sufficient to cover the other expenses. What then can be done to remedy the situation?

In managing your money, two things and only two things can be done to improve *any* budget squeeze: you can increase the income or decrease the outgo. Obviously, if there is not enough money to cover all "must" expenses, income is going to need a boost at least temporarily. The important thing to realize, however, is that even if it does become necessary for a wife to take a short term job or for a husband to take a moonlighting job, these things should be considered only as emergency measures to be used strictly for applying the money to the elimination of "must" bills. Under no circumstances should one cent of the emergency income be allowed to creep into other categories of the budget, because, in doing so, the family may unconsciously raise its standard of living to the point where it will be necessary to continue with the emergency second income forever.

The other method of dealing with ends that don't meet is by cutting expenses. As the outgo decreases, the income, without having changed, reaches the point of being adequate to cover expenses.

Most of us can cut expenses if we have to do so, even if our present lifestyle is more enjoyable. We *like* setting the thermostat at seventy degrees instead of sixty-two in the winter. We *like* buying magazines instead of reading them for free at the public library. We *like* taking long rides through the countryside even if gasoline prices are astronomical. Yet the comment I hear most frequently from financially strapped women is, "I've cut my expenses to the bone! There's not another expense I can eliminate!" The truth is, what most of us consider "cut to the bone" would be luxury in the eyes of the greatest portion of the world's population. It is quite unlikely there exists any budget which is truly as lean as it could be in an absolute pinch. Of course, I'm not advocating unmerciful austerity, but a second look at the budget may provide new ideas for some additional trimming.

For instance, I've always thought of myself as a fairly careful money manager, yet when a real financial emergency arose I was astonished to discover just how much my budget could be pared. Because of the combined factors of illness, dental bills, car repair bills, rising prices, and a slight cut in income, we found ourselves overwhelmed by financial problems. After a serious look at the budget, it was evident that some drastic means must be devised for coping with the problem. Since no extra income was available, we had to cut the outgo.

Have you ever given yourself or anyone else a haircut? Neither had I, but I learned and saved the money my daughter and I were spending on trims every other month. Are you letting money "dribble" away? We were. By eliminating magazine purchases and listening to radio news instead of buying a newspaper we were stunned at the amount of savings. Are you using too much gasoline by making needless trips to the store? I was, and by restricting myself to getting all the errands done in one trip I cut my gasoline consumption by one-third.

Certainly some of these methods do seem drastic, but at times drastic measures are the only ones that work. A dollar here and a quarter there doesn't sound like much when considered individually, but when lumped together into a fifty dollars a month savings those dollars and quarters can make a difference.

Jesus at one time used budgets as an illustration of a point He was making about discipleship. To make His meaning clear, He used the example of pre-planning according to available income:

> For which of you, intending to build a tower, sitteth not down first, and counteth the cost, whether he have sufficient to finish it? Lest haply, after he hath laid the foundation, and is not able to finish it, all that behold it begin to mock him, saying, This man began to build, and was not able to finish (Luke 14:28-30).

Planning well, and then continuing in accordance with that plan is the only way to escape financial woes.

The Management of Necessary Expense

There is not a great deal you can do about the bills to which you have already committed yourself. The car payment, the mortgage, and your health insurance are fairly fixed expenses. These things are the unavoidable bites out of your income. Other equally unavoidable expenditures are such things as utility bills, medical expenses, and school lunch money. These things can be manipulated to a certain extent, but even if they are trimmed they still exist. Eradicate the installment payments you are making as soon as you can. No stable financial base can be built on the misuse of credit.

Having the obvious expenses out of the way, you are left with such things as grocery money, gasoline money, school money, and money for the paper boy, the barber, and the Avon lady. Typically, when all these things are subtracted from the remaining funds not much remains for savings, entertainment, gift giving, unexpected repair bills, eating out occasionally, annual payments of car insurance, license plates, and taxes. How can we possibly budget in so many directions?

The answer lies in setting more priorities. The temptation is to put every available cent into paying the current bills in an effort to rid ourselves of them. In order to spread the money in all the directions it must go, bill paying day may leave the checking account with no money left for other vital expenses. As a consequence it becomes necessary to skimp on the groceries and maybe even resort to charging the gasoline necessary for the days left before the next paycheck comes in. While it is commendable to apply as much cash as possible to the paying off of troublesome installment payments, it is not commendable to do so at the expense of having to resort to making even more charges.

Most women who are having trouble with the finances take the obvious step of juggling the grocery money. Of all the items to be paid this is the one most women think of as being the most flexible. But is it really?

Few Americans have had the experience of going without food entirely, but in many homes the food on the table is of poor quality and variety. Since energy and good health are two of the most valuable assets anyone can possess, does it really save money to stint on the grocery allowance?

Certainly it is possible to eat well on a small food budget, but too many people don't know enough about nutrition to make this happen. Their money is spent, not for low cost protein food such as beans, cheese, or eggs, but for an increase in starches and carbohydrates. Inevitably, the price of ignoring the body's demands for proper fuel will have to be met. It is senseless to save money on groceries if the only way one knows how to do so is by creating less than nutritious meals, which, in the long run, will only cause expenditures for medical and dental treatments.

The first step then in bringing the grocery expense into line is to learn everything you can about nutrition in order to save money. Anyone can serve a balanced meal when she has the funds for an ample roast, fresh vegetables, specialty breads, and out of season fresh fruit. The challenge comes when she doesn't have the funds for that kind of fare, yet must still meet her family's nutritional needs.

Since the family health is such a vital issue, the grocery allowance should receive primary attention. After tithes have been paid and the mortgage and utility bills taken out, the grocery money should come next. This is not to suggest that an outrageous amount be spent on groceries, but rather that you set aside a reasonable amount of grocery money and then use it for that purpose even if doing so means paying only a minimum amount on some installment loan bill.

Two other expenditures should also be taken care of before applying money to other expenses—gasoline money and your "running" money. (My husband calls this the "running" money because he says it is what we use to run our family on from one payday until the next.) You know gasoline expenses will have to come out of each paycheck, but, unless you set aside a specific amount for this purpose immediately, it may be spent in other ways and you will be left with no alternative other than resorting to the use of credit cards. And you can't get yourself out of debt by creating new charges while you are struggling to pay off old ones.

"Running" money is another essential which can only result in problems if you don't set aside a specific amount before all your available funds are used elsewhere. Nobody can get by without a certain amount of small expenses which nibble away at the budget. You will be able to curtail considerably in this area, but don't make the mistake of assuming you can get by without any "running" money at all. If you try this, you will wind up having to borrow necessary funds from another allotment, which in turn will make it necessary to readjust still another budget category. Once this chain starts your entire budget will be in ruins. Rather than face this, start off by allotting yourself a realistic amount of money to cover the small expenses which inevitably crop up. No two families will have quite the same circumstances in this area so you will have to judge for yourself how much you will need after taking into consideration such things as buying newspapers, getting a haircut, putting a dollar into the Salvation Army kettle at Christmas, buying your mother a birthday card, giving your children their allowances and lunch money, paying your club dues, chipping in on a friend's going away present, or paying parking fees. Certainly the category of "running" money presents a real opportunity for trimming the budget because many of the things we spend money on in this way may be unnecessary. Only you can decide which things are to be eliminated.

Another priority, if at all possible, is personal spending money. If you are up against a wall financially, you will want to exercise moderation here, but, if possible, allot yourself something that you can spend without having to account for it to anyone. The amount you set aside here can be whatever you can reasonably afford, but don't get carried away. The purpose of this spending money is to make you feel good about having some "free" money and the amount is not important. If, however, you are putting the price of a new purse or a pair of gold earrings into this fund each week that is overdoing it. Try for a more realistic figure. At times my own finances have been so strained that the price of a magazine was all I could afford for my personal spending, yet simply having the money, even though the sum was small, made me feel less like a candidate for the poor house.

"Owe No Man"

After the tithes, mortgage, utilities, food, gasoline, running money, and personal expense money are taken care of, then comes the payment of other obligations such as clothing, installment loans, medical bills, and insurance payments. The first financial goal any Christian woman should set for herself is to be free of debt. Indebtedness is contrary to Scripture, and the family who truly desires to serve the Lord in all areas should concentrate their most intense efforts on eliminating debts. The word *owe* is used only one time in the Bible and in that use we are told *not* to owe. "Owe no man any thing, but to love one another. . ." (Romans 13:8).

While most of us must live with mortgaged homes, we don't have to live with mortgaged gasoline and mortgaged clothing. The biggest threat to any family's peace of mind is the undisciplined use of credit.

If you and your family have made the mistake of falling into the credit trap, by all means make an all out-effort to extricate yourself. The installment plan not only wrecks your budget but it can also wreck your peace of mind and even your Christian testimony. The world has the "gimme" attitude and as Christians we have a responsibility to show the difference Christ has made in our lives.

Can you effectively witness to your neighbor when she sees you are just as greedy for "things" as she is? How can you show her that Christ gives contentment when, like her, you are busily buying everything in sight on the installment plan? Certainly emergencies do occur and many Christians find themselves in financial trouble which is not of their own making, but the majority of those who are frantically juggling two jobs and dealing with impatient creditors are those who have allowed their faith in a piece of plastic to take precedence over their faith in God's ability to provide for their needs.

If you have allowed yourself to be enveloped in the tangle of installment debts, why not commit your finances right now into God's hands and resolve that, with His help, you will clear your financial slate and will learn from past mistakes.

Turning your financial problems over to God is the *only* way to effectively sort them out, but in committing your troubles to Him, don't make the mistake of assuming that this lets you off the hook with creditors. Christians have an obligation to pay what they owe. If you have made a debt, then live up to its demands. Don't try to use religion as a wall to hide behind to escape your obligations. The miracle God works is not in letting you slip out of your responsibilities, but rather in transforming your motives and actions. Trust Him to change you and then with His help and guidance your financial situation will change accordingly.

During the Depression a popular slogan was often quoted. To those who are serious about getting out of debt, this slogan might well be a good reminder of the way to stay out of debt in the future: "Use it up. Wear it out. Make it do."

If you are truly serious about improving your finances, depend on God and then put your own initiative to work in the ways this slogan suggests. Eliminate wastefulness. Get the full benefit from each purchase, and don't buy things you really don't need.

The Leftovers Everybody Likes

Leftovers are not fashionable. Indeed, the term is being eliminated entirely; leftovers are given a new dignity by being called "recycled." Yet there is one leftover that will never prove unpopular and that is leftover money. I have frequently heard complaints about too much month left over at the end of the money, but I have never heard a complaint about too much money left over at the end of the month.

Theoretically, no one should have any left-over money. According to the experts, money plans are supposed to be so well defined that the only unaccounted for nickel in your pocket is the one you found five minutes ago on the sidewalk. However, life doesn't operate according to experts' theories. Once you get a workable budget and debts are eliminated, you may start to accumulate "leftovers." The priority, then, is to channel those leftovers in the right direction. Undisciplined leftovers can lull you into thinking you have more cash to deal with than you actually do and can result in a subtle raising of the family standard of living, which, in its turn, results in a return to the old habit of living from payday to payday.

What then can be done with the leftovers? Anything you wish as long as you use them in such a way that does not jeopardize the future of your budget. The possibly wisest use of leftovers is the investing of them as a means of fighting tomorrow's inflation. This is done by buying now that product which you will require later but which is most assuredly going to rise in price. For example, let's suppose it is the end of March and you are in a department store. You discover that winter coat prices have been slashed drastically. You find a coat just the right size and color and the price is reduced 40 percent. Your current winter coat is ready to be discarded, and you plan to buy a new coat for the coming winter. Buying that coat could be an extremely wise investment of your leftover money, because, by the time winter rolls around, a similar coat will cost the original price plus 10 percent or more. By purchasing the coat on sale at 40 percent you may have saved yourself 50 percent of the price you would be paying later in the year.

In situations where spending for something you are going to need later makes it possible for you to make spectacular savings, your money will have actually worked for you more efficiently than it would have had you put it in a savings account. There it would have gained you perhaps as little as 6 percent, while, by spending wisely, you were able to make a gain of 50 percent on your investment.

If this seems out of line with Grandpa's axiom that saving money for a rainy day was all important, then you will need to realize that your grandparents may never have known times of double-digit inflation. I am not suggesting that savings are not worthwhile. Certainly everyone needs some money to fall back on in case of an emergency. However, the rule of putting your money in a savings account until some long-term goal is accomplished is no longer applicable. A better idea is to save only until enough funds are accrued to enable you to switch over to a means of drawing higher interest. Short-term savings certificates offer a means of doing this. Right now the minimum investment necessary for these certificates is one thousand dollars, and you have to forfeit a portion of your interest if you hold the certificates less than the specified time, which is usually six months. Then if your leftovers are really spectacular, you may want to buy Treasury notes. The least you can invest here is ten thousand dollars, but Treasury notes are a good idea if you inherit or otherwise happen to come into a large sum of money and want to get more than a savings account can offer.

While the majority of us are never going to be confronted with the problem of having more money than we need, you may happen to be blessed with this difficulty at some future date. If so, why not consider investing that surplus in something that yields more than financial rewards?

Hoarding money is contrary to Scripture. Remember the unprofitable servant who hid his talent in the ground rather than using it to its full potential? So it is with the Christian's money. God knows that all of us have needs but He expects us to trust Him for those needs. When a Christian starts putting away every available dime he shows a lack of trust in God's providing ability. A sensible amount of savings is good money management and the Lord commends wise use of assets (see Luke 16:1-12). To pile up dollars, however—not for specific purposes but rather for the greedy pleasure derived from simply having them—is not in the best interest of any believer.

Have you instead considered investing your leftovers in

missions or other worthwhile Christian endeavors? Jesus instructed:

> Lay not up for yourselves treasures upon earth, where moth and rust doth corrupt, and where thieves break through and steal: but lay up for yourselves treasures in heaven, where neither moth nor rust doth corrupt, and where thieves do not break through nor steal: for where your treasure is, there will your heart be also (Matt. 6:19-21).

Eliminating Bad Spending Habits

"I Really Shouldn't Have!"

The only thing worse than knowing someone has conned you into buying something you couldn't afford or didn't need is knowing that you conned yourself into doing it. When it comes to bad spending habits most of us are our own worst enemies.

Have you ever returned home with a purchase only to discover that the dress that looked so flattering in the store really didn't do much for you once you were out of the range of the salesclerk's flattering remarks?

Or have you ever yielded to a friend's insistence that you accompany her on a shopping trip even though you knew you couldn't afford to spend any money—and you did it anyway?

Or have you ever been to a jewelry party or a plastics party or a cleaning products party and found yourself ordering things that you didn't really want and certainly couldn't afford?

Everybody spends money unwisely at times. Yet many people suffer more from the malady than the average person does. For the "victim," a dollar in the purse or even a credit card in the purse, is an invitation to indulgence. These spenders don't care what they buy as long as they can buy something. While a person who is a compulsive spender may need professional counseling, the rest of us can benefit by an application of common sense. By seeking out our problem areas and knowing our weaknesses, we can learn to tighten up on them.

The first thing to do is learn why the unwise spending took place. Was the shopping trip purposeful or was it merely for the sake of passing time? Shopping as a means of relieving boredom is dangerous to the budget. Was the purchase made to save face in front of friends or salesclerks? Again we come back to the problem of attitude and self-image. Nobody wants to be thought of as a skinflint. Was the purchase made as an aid to combat depression or money worries? Ironically, some of the people who are the deepest in debt are those who use buying as a means of cheering themselves up temporarily.

To see where your problem areas are, try making a chart of your "shouldn't have" purchases for a few weeks and the results will no doubt surprise you. You may discover that money is not your real problem at all, but rather boredom, or a low sense of self-worth, which makes you constantly strive to be noticed by others.

Each time you buy something which you later decide was unnecessary, overpriced, or even unwanted, write down the circumstances under which the purchase was made. When did it happen? Who were you with? Why were you in the store? As the weeks pass, you will begin to see a pattern emerge and as you get to the root of the problem and learn exactly what your weakness is, you will be able to develop a workable plan for avoiding the temptation.

Temptation on the Party Plan

Unless a woman spends her entire adult life in Antarctica she will receive invitations to "parties." Thinly disguised as social functions these get-togethers are just another way of reaching potential buyers. Of course, the hostess will serve refreshments and you will play a few amusing games, but the real purpose of the party is selling. Only a genuinely budget-conscious woman can attend one of these parties and leave without spending money she didn't intend to spend.

The problem here is not the seller. After all, you know before you set foot in the door that goods are going to be offered for sale. The problem isn't usually the product either; most of the jewelry, cosmetics, plastics, and cleaning products are of dependable quality. Neither does the problem lie with your friend who is giving the party, because most likely when she invited you she made it quite clear that she is seeking enough sales to get that cookware set she wants. The real problem is not the party, but the party goer. It is terribly hard not to get caught up in the sales pitch and the desire to help your friend.

As a full-time stay-at-home wife and mother I had my share—and yours—of party invitations. I have attended them, bought things I didn't want or couldn't afford, and then felt disgusted with myself. I have also attended them, bought things I could afford and use and felt pleased with the purchase. For me, the big difference was in learning how to deal with the parties.

In the first place, if you can't buy anything or don't want anything it is probably best not to go to the party at all. I make it a policy to always insist on looking over the catalog before agreeing to attend the party. Then if I see that the items are overpriced or of no interest to me, I stay at home, because going to the party without buying is difficult. The dealer will tell you that you don't have to pay a cent until the product comes in a few weeks later, so pleading temporary insolvency won't help. "Oh, but you'll be getting another payday before the order comes in," the dealer will assure you cheerfully.

Parties can be fun, but if they are getting to be too much of a temptation for you, stay home.

Looking for Unnecessary Bargains

At one time I ran a dressmaking business and one of my customers was the wife of a well-to-do businessman. Although the family was quite comfortable financially the woman was constantly trying to get "bargains." Her favorite topic of conversation was a discourse on the horrible prices charged at the supermarket. Every time she paid me she acted as though pulling the money from her wallet was physical torture. I thought at first that she must be the most dedicated penny pincher I had ever met. Then one day I revised my opinion.

"You ought to go down to Penney's and buy some hair dryers," she told me excitedly one day when she came for a fitting.

"I don't need one," I told her.

"Oh, that doesn't matter," she said as she dismissed such a ridiculous thought. "They've got 'em on sale for only ten dollars and you ought to take advantage of the sale and stock up."

I looked at her in total disbelief. I had heard of stocking up on tuna fish or peanut butter or maybe even toothpaste, but hair dryers?

"I bought five of them" she continued enthusiastically.

"Whatever are you going to do with *five* hairdryers? Even if they were giving them away, why would you need five of them?"

She shrugged. "I don't know, but they were such a bargain! I put them up in the attic and I'll think of something to do with them sometime."

That was six years ago. If I could peek into her attic today I suspect I would still find five hair dryers packed away there.

The problem for many of us is that we have become so acutely bargain conscious that we tend to snatch up anything that is offered at a wonderfully low price, regardless of whether we need it or not. Is a low-priced object which we don't need a real bargain? Not at all! A real bargain is something of good quality that has an appealing price and is needed or wanted.

Most of us have at one time or another gotten carried away just as my friend did with the five hair dryers. It is not a good feeling to realize later that your "bargain" wasn't such a bargain after all, but it is a feeling most of us have shared. Chapter Five tells how you can determine if a sale priced item is a genuine bargain.

Buying Is Not a Tranquilizer

A couple whom we were once closely acquainted with were in severe financial trouble. The wife had a mysterious ailment which several doctors had been unable to diagnose. Medical bills began to pile up. The couple looked around to find ways of cutting expenses and could find no way. They were committed to house payments, installment furniture payments, car notes, and revolving charge accounts. Without the illness they were barely making it from payday to payday.

I tried to visit my friend as often as possible because I knew she was depressed over both her health and the family finances. Each time I visited she told me repeatedly of how desperate the situation was becoming and I tried to help by offering a sympathetic ear. She told me she had pared expenses to the bone, and I encouraged her in her penny-pinching.

Then on Easter morning when I arrived at church I had quite a shock. My friend was all dressed up in Easter finery from head to toe. I couldn't believe my eyes! Where did she get the money for that kind of outfit when she could barely buy groceries? Later in the week as I talked to her she admitted that she had omitted paying a bill in order to finance her elegant clothing.

"I think it's important to keep your spirits up when you're having hard times," she explained. "Nothing cheers me up like new clothes do."

About two weeks later, during a visit she led me to the bedroom to see her latest purchase. To my surprise she had completely redone the room with new drapes, new bedspread, and even carpeting.

"Not having enough money to pay the bills depresses me," she confided, "so I decided to re-do my bedroom and cheer myself up."

Within a few months there was nothing my friend could buy to cheer herself up enough to forget reality. The family had lost its home and many of its other belongings, and both husband and wife were under medical treatment and taking tranquilizers to help them get through the emotionally destructive ordeal of bankruptcy.

The ironic thing is that my friend is not unintelligent. Nor is she in the minority when it comes to the principle of "buying something new to cheer myself up." Credit counselors who work with those trying to avoid bankruptcy and lawyers who work with couples filing bankruptcy find unwise buying when in desperate financial straits to be almost the rule rather than the exception.

Impulsive use of buying as a tranquilizer is not only futile but leads ultimately to further depression. Making do without a new Easter outfit and nice home furnishings may be somewhat depressing to some people but in no way can it compare with the major depression of losing a home and all other belongings. "Things" cannot provide lasting happiness:

> And whatsoever mine eyes desired I kept not from them, I withheld not my heart from any joy; for my heart rejoiced in all my labour: and this was my portion of all my labour. Then I looked on all the works that my hands had wrought, and on the labour that I had laboured to do: and behold, all

> was vanity and vexation of spirit, and there was no profit under the sun (Eccles. 2:10-11).

The wise preacher came to understand that regardless of how much he accumulated, true joy could be found only in God, and the heaping up of earthly treasures was a vanity to be left to sinners:

> For God giveth to a man that is good in his sight wisdom, and knowledge, and joy: but to the sinner he giveth travail, to gather and to heap up, that he may give to him that is good before God. This also is vanity and vexation of spirit (Eccles. 2:26).

Inability to Say No

In his book, *John Plowman's Talks*, Charles Spurgeon gave a piece of advice, which, if heeded, can eliminate most of the financial problems Christians suffer. His advice was, "Learn to say no and it will do you more good than being able to speak Latin."

What makes this simple word so difficult to say? Are we afraid of being thought a spoilsport, a Scrooge, or a religious fanatic?

The primary reason most people buy things they neither want or need lies in their inability to say no. Admittedly, it is difficult to frame this word when the person who is enticing you is someone you love. Consequently, most children have a roomful of toys, games, clothes, and electronic gadgets their parents never meant to buy for them in the first place.

Likewise it is hard to say no to a friend. How do you tell the person who is peddling cosmetics or handmade quilts that you simply don't want her wares? Of course, you can't come right out and say that, so rather than admit the truth you buy.

That same friend can influence you on a shopping trip, too. Certainly she isn't going to pressure you into buying things she has no monetary stake in, but doesn't her presence exert a subtle influence on your decisions? If she is spending freely you will feel like the worst kind of tightwad if you spend the day browsing. Unintentionally, your friend *does* exert pressure on your shopping habits and good budgeting sense. It is especially difficult to say no when others are saying yes.

A persuasive salesperson is the most difficult of all to resist. Those who are well trained in their profession know how to motivate you to sell the item to yourself. In high quality stores no clerk would dream of exercising obvious pressure upon you. Instead, with a slightly tilted head, a raised eyebrow, and a knowing look, she is capable of extracting a sale from you without a word because she knows that you feel a refusal to buy will be a loss of face for you. She understands that nobody wants anything as much as a good self-image.

The ability to say no sometimes is needed in situations involving more than buying. Frequently mothers, in particular, are called upon to perform chores which to the casual observer seem not to involve money at all, but which are in reality dreadfully expensive. Good causes that ask only for your time may in the long run be the most expense making area of your life. For example, when my daughter was a first grader, I became involved with Camp Fire Girls. On the surface, meeting with eight little girls once a week to work with pine cones and paste and skits and songs doesn't seem to be expensive at all. But I calculated that, even in 1974, the cost of being a Blue Bird leader was approximately ten dollars per week. I'm not against good causes and I thoroughly enjoyed my little Blue Birds, but the point I'm making is that before saying yes to any worthwhile cause it is a good idea to see if your budget can take on refreshments, gasoline, paste, carpet repairs, and the price of last-minute convenience foods you'll need because you didn't have time to cook.

Since saying no is so difficult for all of us, is there any practical way of learning to refuse to part with our money when we don't want to buy what we are being pressured to buy? Yes, saying no can be learned. The first thing to realize is that "no" is enough. You don't have to explain, apologize, or rationalize. Doing any of those things leaves you open to a further sales pitch or exerting of influence. Let's say you attend a plastics party and you tell your hostess, "No, I really can't buy anything. I'm a little broke right now." You have left yourself open for her to say, "Oh, but the order won't be back for two weeks." Then you change tactics and say, "But I already have all the storage containers I need." Her toe goes in the door immediately as she counters with, "But they make such wonderful gifts!" You respond by saying, "I don't know anyone I'll be giving a gift to in the near future." Then she advises confidentially, "It's a good idea to buy some things and tuck them away. You never know when you might get an unexpected wedding invitation." The result? Your no doesn't stick and you are left with a hole in your budget.

The *only* way to effectively say no is to say it and stop there. After you have politely said, "No thanks" and looked appropriately disinterested it is a rare person who will say, "Why not?" For that, I have another answer: "Because." If anything is harder to argue with than "no," it is "because"!

Everybody Has to Eat

Women and Groceries

Since the time of Eve, grocery shopping and preparation are chores which have traditionally fallen into the hands of women. Even the first recorded biblical conversation in which Eve took part began with a discussion of food. But given a choice of all the foods in the Garden of Eden, Eve made an unwise decision.

While no other food-selecting experience could ever again have the disastrous results of that one, Eve's descendants have often been guilty of making unwise food selections. And just as Eve was not the only one who suffered for her bad judgment, today's grocery buyer also causes others to suffer for her inappropriate choosing.

Since buying the family's food has traditionally been the responsibility of the woman of the household, this chore has always represented a real opportunity for developing good stewardship. Even the wife who has no control over other areas of the family finances, usually has the final say in grocery shopping.

As a matter of fact, the woman who can competently handle grocery shopping is commended in the Bible. In the description of the virtuous woman a reference is made to her acquiring of food: "She is like the merchants' ships; she bringeth her food from afar" (Prov. 31:14). It seems that the virtuous woman practiced comparison shopping and careful selectivity.

Throughout the Bible references are made to eating and drinking and to the fact that both are meant to be enjoyed. In Ecclesiastes this fact is reiterated five times. "There is nothing better for a man, than that he should eat and drink, and that he should make his soul enjoy good in his labour. This also I saw, that it was from the hand of God" (Eccles. 2:24).

Attitude Counts

To the woman in search of solid help with her grocery budget, nothing counts as much as her attitude. If you think you are defeated by inflation's effect on grocery prices, then you probably are. Only when you decide that the results are worth the effort involved in the fight can you successfully reduce your output of grocery dollars.

Perhaps the best way to develop an appropriate attitude toward grocery shopping is to see it as a means of manifesting some of your Christian principles. Good handling of the grocery budget allows you to express yourself through stewardship, good health, Christian example, and moderation.

Stewardship is the handling of whatever you have, whether it be education, a good singing voice, or the twenty dollars you are spending on groceries, in a manner that pleases God and brings honor to Him. If you think He isn't interested in your grocery-buying problems, try reading I Kings 17:12-16.

Good health enables the Christian to more effectively work for the Lord, and what better way can a wife and mother equip her family with the physical strength for service than by feeding them wisely? Just as Daniel and his fellow captives chose to eat healthful food rather than the king's food, even so should the woman who buys groceries seek to provide the best possible nutrition with the amount of money she has to spend. Daniel and his friends ate pulse, which is beans and peas, and grew healthy and strong on this diet; see Daniel 1:8-16.

Christian example is shown to the world by exhibiting God-given wisdom. In Proverbs the example of the lowly ant's food gathering habits is used to point out the wisdom of industriousness: "Go to the ant, thou sluggard; consider her ways, and be wise: which having no guide, overseer, or ruler, provideth her meat in the summer, and gathereth her food in the harvest" (Prov. 6:6-8). If an insect can be commended for her wisdom in regard to food gathering, can any believer afford to do less than the ant?

Moderation can be exhibited through good stewardship of grocery money. While food is essential to life, it is not becoming to a Christian's testimony to overindulge in eating. The Bible shows gluttony and drunkenness as leading to the same end: "For the drunkard and the glutton shall come to poverty . . ." (Prov. 23:21). The apostle Paul in writing to the Philippians also warned of the dire consequences of putting the act of eating ahead of the service of God (Phil. 3:19).

Once a Christian sees her spending in the light of stewardship, it becomes much easier to invest time and effort in becoming an effective shopper and a creative cook. Bargain hunting is time-consuming work. Only by exercising real dedication to the task can anyone possibly hope to come out ahead. If you aren't willing to admit that at the start and to buckle down to the task, then your complaints about prices are nothing more than empty grumbles.

What Does It Cost to Eat?

A young bride who was looking over her financial obligations, complained to her mother, "We could get along just fine if we could figure out how to give up groceries!"

Quite possibly, every woman who has ever bought groceries for her family has, on more than one occasion, had that same thought. With food prices rising by the week it does seem as though the biggest chunk of our budget is being left in the supermarket. It has been estimated that most families with moderate incomes spend at least 25 percent of their total earnings on food alone.

Of all the items in a woman's household budget the area of grocery shopping offers more chance for effective and creative economizing than any other category. The key lies in a willingness to invest time learning more about food, money—and yourself.

Many argue that comparison shopping is a waste of time now that gasoline has become so costly. However, this argument won't stand up under close inspection. As long as your grocery buying excursions use less than a gallon of gasoline you are probably getting a bargain by comparison shopping. With a diligent effort anyone can cut her grocery bill as much as 10 percent through comparison shopping without changing her grocery list. For those more adventurous shoppers who are willing to experiment with substitutions, house brands, and meatless meals, a savings of up to 25 percent is a reasonable expectation.

One time, as a personal experiment for an article I was writing for a magazine, I compiled food prices based on the theory that shopping in only one store is more economical. Nothing could have been further from the truth. To my astonishment, I found it possible to save as much as five dollars at each store by sticking with the advertised bargains. A savings of five dollars at each store more than offset the price of the gallon of gasoline required for shopping in more than one location. I also noted that grocery stores tend to be in clusters anyway. In my own neighborhood six chain stores compete with each other on the same highway, and the distance between the first store and the last is only one mile.

Groceries are the one inescapable item on your budget. The only consolation is that, while we can't eliminate the expenditure, we can reshape it and, maybe in the process, learn to enjoy the game of trying to outwit inflation.

Your Family and Their Effect on the Grocery Budget

How does your family feel about the grocery budget? Are they willing to work with you by not demanding expensive items which wipe out your shopping gains? If not, then re-educating your family will have to be your first priority in bringing your grocery spending under control.

If necessary, take your husband grocery shopping with you so that he can see for himself the difference between the cost of a pound of hamburger and a pound of T-bone steak. Ask your teenagers to help in compiling menus that are tasty, nutritious, and economical. Since teens consume more food than any other age group, your real budget bite may come in keeping your husky sons well fueled. If, while discussing menus, you can appeal to your son's desire for muscles and your daughter's interest in slimness and an acne-free complexion, you may get their cooperation.

For younger children, attitude changing is much less complicated. If they are under three years old, they are still fairly adaptable and their attitude can be molded. If they are from three to twelve, they have probably already become used to certain eating patterns, but they are still young enough to change if dealt with in a decisive manner. Since children are eager to do what they consider grown-up activities, you might find it helps to involve them in both the shopping and meal preparation. Most children will eat practically anything they help to cook, and if hamburger casserole has not previously gotten rave reviews at your house, try letting your ten-year-old put it together. Her attitude will probably be quite different.

Some women have had success in changing family shopping habits by letting their children share in the rewards of cutting the grocery expenditures. The program works like this: Set a realistic budget figure, one that is neither excessive nor unreasonably stingy. Then challenge the children to help you gain leftover grocery money and allow them to keep the surplus. If you have planned realistically, they won't get enough surplus to cause problems, but they will get enough to encourage them to scour through magazines for cents-off coupons and to eat budget meals without complaining. Of course, you are thinking that letting the children keep the surplus is not going to help your budget, and to a certain extent that is true. In most cases, however, children won't stay interested in the game for more than a few months, so your investment in their attitude changes won't be astronomically expensive. Meanwhile you will have re-educated their eating habits and as a consequence you can continue to serve the economical meals to which they have become accustomed.

Changing Lifestyles Add to Food Costs

We have come a long way since the days when families raised most of their own food and were completely self-sufficient. Not only do we buy more than our grandparents did, but we insist upon a more exotic choice of food and a built-in ease of preparation. These two factors, along with the more complicated ones of inflation and the increase in middlemen, have driven prices steadily upward. We take for granted Mexican strawberries, California avocadoes, Florida oranges, and Hawaiian pineapples. For most of us these things are no longer special treats, but are things we expect to see in the grocery stores. The increasing sophistication of both our eating and shopping habits have had a radical effect on prices.

Convenience foods are no longer regarded as luxury items. Cake mixes, frozen foods, and ready-to-eat items comprise a healthy percentage of the market basket total.

Through the bombardment of advertising we have become conditioned to think that we "deserve" the luxury of convenience foods, but the cook on a budget will find it a great savings to re-orientate her thinking. While convenience foods do have a place and should be utilized at times, cooking from scratch is still, in many cases, the most effective means of cutting food costs. Sometimes scratch cooking is not all that involved. For example, on your next trip to the supermarket compare the price of vegetables frozen in butter sauce with those frozen plain and with fresh ones in the produce section. Depending on the season, the frozen ones may be the cheapest, but inevitably the package containing the butter sauce will cost a great deal more. The amount of time, energy, and cost involved in adding your own pat of butter is much less than the 50 percent surcharge for the already buttered vegetables.

In determining whether convenience foods should have their place in your grocery cupboard, be willing to experiment. Weigh such factors as time and effort involved in preparing the scratch equivalent. If only a few cents difference exists, the convenience food may be a good buy *if* you are willing to use the time it saves you in creating another scratch dish which shows a marked savings over the price of its convenience counterpart.

As far as out-of-season fruits and vegetables are concerned, a basic knowledge of nutrition can save you a great deal of money. If you know which foods provide which nutrients you can put balanced meals on the table all year round by buying in-season foods. For instance, now that food can be readily flown from one country to another, both apples and green beans can be had fresh just about anytime you want them. However, August, September, and October are the peak months for apples and July and August are the peak months for green beans. This means that during those months these two items will generally be both plentiful and low in cost. If you really want to trim your grocery budget learn to utilize both nutrition facts and a knowledge of peak seasons for various fruits and vegetables. Does it make sense to pay high prices for apples when low-cost cantaloupes are in season? Not if you know your nutrition facts. Cantaloupes far exceed apples in nutritional value. Likewise, does it pay to serve out-of-season green beans just for the sake of having something fresh and green on the table? Not if you know that the much lower priced greens, such as collards and turnip greens, are higher in nutritional value.

If you don't know which foods offer the most nutrition for the least amount of money, find out. If you need more information than your public library can provide, write to the Superintendent of Documents, U.S. Printing Office, Washington, D.C. 20402, and ask for help. The government prints thousands of booklets on every imaginable subject, and the information is first-rate. List the subject you are interested in, and you will be notified what is available and how much it costs. For a small fee you can receive booklets on virtually any aspect of food shopping that puzzles you.

In addition to our acceptance of convenience foods and out-of-season food, Americans have developed some other changes in their lifestyles which may also have a considerable influence on food budgets. The greatest change in eating habits is that families are moving away from traditional sit-down meals. In many homes the family only eats together once or twice a week and then it is at irregular times. Meal skipping is prevalent as is eating out, snacking on junk food, and eating on the constant nibble plan. Does your family eat breakfast and supper together during the week? If so, are these full course, nutritionally prepared meals, served at specific times? For most families the answer to both questions is no, and these changing lifestyles are taking their toll on the family food budget.

It costs a great deal more to have your family grab instant breakfast bars on the run than it does to offer them a nutritionally adequate breakfast. It also costs a great deal more to have food preparation going on at all hours than it does to serve one meal. Not only is energy wasted in numerous uses of the oven or grill but also food. Food waste is more easily controlled by serving meals at specific times.

Perhaps the most significant factor in our changing grocery bills is the desire for tantalizing tastes. Just about everybody eats too much salt and sugar and it shows not only in our health but in our budget. Potato chips, pretzels, cookies, sweet drinks, and other non-nutritional foods take a hefty percentage of the grocery funds.

The high prices Americans are paying for their changing lifestyles are not only measured in dollars. Right now, this country is setting new records for heart disease, high blood pressure, obesity, and diabetes. Your desire to save money at the grocery store could at the same time become a means of giving your family a better life.

The real question, then, is not whether you want to cut your grocery budget, but whether you are willing to change your lifestyle, because this is the only genuinely effective way that you can achieve lasting effects on your budget.

How to Do It

1. Decide who is going to be in charge. Do you *really* control the grocery buying, or are you simply the person who puts the items in the cart and pays for them? In most homes, each family member demands what they want and the only real decision the mother has left to her is whether to buy plain flour or self-rising. To get your budget in line, you must take charge. If cutting off the supply of soft drinks or snack goodies raises the roof, let the children have them as long as they buy them out of their allowance and not out of your grocery budget. Letting a child finance his own wants is the quickest way I know to teach him the difference between wants and needs, and soon that bag of potato chips that costs half of his week's allowance won't look nearly so appealing.

Being in charge also means you will shop with a list made by you after inventorying the supplies already on hand. Inventories and lists are useless if everybody in the household feels free to scribble their own additions onto your carefully planned list.

Being in charge also means exercising control over your kitchen. Does your family wander into the kitchen any time they choose and take any food item out that catches their eye? If so, getting them to change their ways is a must. The three frankfurters your son consumes as an afternoon snack could have been an addition to a meal for all of you. By adding those three frankfurters to a large can of pork and beans and seasoning it with onion, molasses, vinegar, and worcestershire sauce you could have served a budget pleasing dinner. After Junior gets through foraging, however, you will have to make a trip to the store and possibly overpay as a result of having to grab quickly rather than selectively. If your family is in the habit of rambling through the kitchen and munching on whatever they find, put a stop to it immediately. Provide some snacks, such as apples, oranges, raisins, or sunflower seeds, and let the family know these things can be eaten at appropriate snack times without asking permission. All other food items, however, must be cleared first with you. If you are appalled by this suggestion, remember this: It is *your* kitchen, isn't it? You are in charge, aren't you?

2. Do your homework. What's the difference in cost between homemade muffins and those made from a mix? What's the price per serving of the brand of canned peas you are currently using? Who is having a sale on detergent this week? What did you do with those cents-off coupons you clipped yesterday? Only by being prepared to answer questions such as these can you be prepared for a grocery buying expedition, yet many women walk into a store without a list or knowledge of sales or cost per servings and expect to save money.

The dedicated budget trimmer should prepare for her grocery buying just as carefully as a general prepares for battle. She should first inventory her supplies and make note of items needed. Then by studying the grocery ads—and *study* is the key word—she should have a good idea of where she will be going to get each item. A separate list should be made for each store. Looking at the grocery ads will guide her in planning the upcoming menus for the week. If chicken is on sale she might decide to substitute chicken and dressing for the company dinner she will be preparing in a few days instead of the beef roast she originally had intended to serve.

Knowing that she has that dish scheduled, she then can note whether or not she needs to add sage and celery to her shopping list.

The next step she takes is to go through her cents-off coupons to see how to most economically use them. Fifty cents off the price of a can of shortening is always nice, but particularly so when the coupon can be used in conjunction with an advertised low price.

After determining exactly where she is going and what she is going to buy, the shopper is ready for action—except for two things. Before leaving home she will eat a good meal to stave off the temptation to impulse buy and then she will go to the store early and alone if possible. Once she is in the store she will concentrate diligently. She will read labels, check nutritional facts, and totally forget brand loyalty. (Any serious shopper should get all those TV jingles out of her head before she goes to the store. If you aren't willing to experiment with lower priced brands, you don't have the right attitude.)

3. Learn the art of creative sneakiness. When buying liquids such as bleach, fabric softener, or milk, look before you snatch. Those bottles are filled by machine and some of them contain an ounce or two more than the others do. Also, if a price on an item has jumped since your last trip, reach to the back of the shelf. Usually there will be a few cans back there that carry the old price.

4. Feed your pet inexpensively. If any of the hungry members of the family is choosy, it is usually the family pet. Cats in particular like to have their say in food selection. However, it is possible to cut your costs considerably here.

Of course, if you have only recently acquired the animal it makes good sense to start him off on inexpensive dry food. However, if the animal has been a member of the family for a while, you definitely have a problem. In spite of those doleful looks cast in your direction, an animal will eat what you serve when he is hungry enough. To make his initial transition easier try mixing the dry food with his regular food or putting a little broth on the food he is disdaining.

If eggs or cheese are on sale, there may be times when it can be quite economical to give your pet a serving of one of these occasionally. It makes a nice change for him and, while it might not be quite as cheap as dry food, it is cheaper than canned food.

Try introducing your pet to vegetables, too. A total meat diet isn't healthy for him anyway and many animals do like vegetables.

5. Don't put more food than you need on the table. Most of us can be readily tempted by the sight of something good to eat. So if you want to cut cost, cut temptation. For example, if you serve pie for dessert, cut it before the meal starts and put it on dessert plates. Then put the remainder of the pie out of sight. If it is on the table, the sight of the pie will prompt requests for seconds. If no seconds are served, you may have enough left over for another meal. Likewise, when serving juice for breakfast, fill the glass and then put the container away.

6. Eat cheap snacks. For the sake of both health and purse it is a good idea to eliminate snacks if you can do so without starting World War III in your own kitchen. If the family can't handle this radical movement without squawking, you might try switching to less costly snacks. Popcorn is about the cheapest and your family can learn to like it without that dangerous coating of too much salt. Also, try sunflower seeds (let your family shell their own—they will eat less that way) or raisins or bananas (a good source of potassium) or saltines and peanut butter.

7. Grocery stores are for buying groceries. Have you ever arrived home after a shopping trip, laden down with grocery sacks and completely out of grocery money, only to discover you still didn't have anything to eat? Perhaps what you actually bought were school supplies, a get-well card for your aunt, a lipstick for your teenage daughter, cold cream for yourself, a magazine for your husband, a model plane kit for your son, some house slippers, a green plant and some fertilizer, plus toothpaste, shoe polish, a turkey roasting pan, and a bottle of aspirin. Sometimes we wonder if we went to the *grocery* store after all.

In most of the instances named above, you could have saved a substantial amount by shopping at either a discount drug store or a discount department store. The *only* things you should be buying with your grocery money are groceries, not toiletries, school supplies, or gifts. Even if you do find a bargain on any of these things at the grocery store—which happens occasionally if the store is having a promotional sale—you should not use your grocery money. Buy it at the grocery store if the price is right, but use either your personal spending money or your funds set aside for gifts or toiletries, *never* your grocery funds. Grocery money is *only* for groceries and the few related cleaning items and paper products you can't get elsewhere at a lower cost. (Discount drug stores and discount chain department stores are often a good source of savings on these items if you can manage an extra stop on your shopping trip.)

*8. **Eliminate or cut back on non-food items.*** Paper products are the most obvious example of unnecessary non-food items. An absorbent dish towel works just as well for mopping up spills, and draining grease through a colander eliminates the use of a paper towel as a grease blotter. Thin, sale-priced terry washcloths make excellent substitutes for paper napkins, and if those aren't nice enough for company, hem a few squares of no-iron remnant material. Encourage the family to use lower cost toilet tissue for nose blowing instead of the more expensive facial tissues. Also, train your family to use only the amount of toilet tissue needed. Children often roll off a long streamer just for the fun of it.

Make your own cleaning products, if possible. A dollop of bleach in the bathroom bowl will clean it as thoroughly as will a high priced special purpose cleaner, but you do have to supply about sixty seconds worth of swishing time. Another savings can be had by cutting back on the amount of product suggested for use by the manufacturer. Often, a half or three-fourths of a cap of dishwashing detergent will do the job just as effectively as will the full recommended amount. Likewise, if your detergent box suggests you use a cup, try using three-fourths of a cup or even seven-eighths. Saving an eighth of a cup of detergent might seem insignificant, but multiplied by a year's worth of washes, the savings does add up.

9. Find inventive ways to cut fruit and vegetable costs. Growing some of your own vegetables can help you save substantially, but if this isn't possible for you there is still an alternative to store bought produce. In many areas of the country, farmers will allow customers to pick their own fruits and vegetables, and, in most cases, doing so saves you as much as 50 percent of the cost, while giving you a chance to enjoy some exercise. If you don't know where to find farms that are operated this way, contact your state agriculture commissioner and he should be able to tell you where to find them.

10. Learn to use coupons creatively. These days it seems everyone is using coupons, but the real savings lies in knowing the best way to use them. Don't use one simply because you happen to have it on hand. Use only those which offer cents off on things you really need. You can make the coupons go even further by waiting to buy the item when it is on sale.

Try to talk your friends into setting up a coupon exchange system with you. That way you can swap the ones you don't need and can get those that you do need.

11. Learn about chemicals. In spite of all the claims made by manufacturers of bleach, window cleaner, and cleansers, there is little difference between the various brands except in the matter of packaging and price. Look at the bottle of bleach you currently use. Most likely it will say, "5 percent sodium hypochlorite, 95 percent inert ingredients." The sodium hypochlorite is the bleaching agent. The other 95 percent is mostly water, or in the case of window cleaners, it may be also perfume and coloring. As soon as you learn the chemical names for the familiar cleaning products you can save yourself quite a bit of money.

The high priced blue window cleaner that contains ammonia and water and a nice smell won't clean a bit better than the cheap green colored one with the same contents. And if you *really* want to save money, buy ammonia instead of the fancy cleaner. That's what does the real work anyway, so why not forego the expense of having it diluted for you and do it yourself.

12. Investigate the old-fashioned practice of bartering. No one ever said that all your grocery bargains have to come from the grocery store. Maybe that neighbor down the street who has more tomatoes than she knows what to do with in her garden would like to swap some of them for your overabundance of green beans. Even if you don't have any green beans maybe a barter is still possible. Can you sew, knit, mow grass, wash windows, or babysit? Or how about helping her can or freeze her crop in return for a share of it?

13. Learn to improvise. With a little experimentation and practice you can learn to make your own convenience items by analyzing the contents and learning to put them together yourself. For instance, a fourth cup of powdered milk plus one teaspoon of sugar and three-fourths of a teaspoon of cocoa gives you the ingredients for hot cocoa mix. All you need add to this mixture is hot water and you have instant cocoa.

Spreadable margarine can be prepared from bulk margarine at a substantial savings. Buy the one pound block and then let it soften up a bit at room temperature. Then add one-half cup of milk and stir until blended. Whip it with your electric mixer until it resembles the fluffy brand you see in the supermarket, for about half the price.

You can make your own maple flavored syrup, too. You need two cups of granulated sugar, one-fourth cup of brown sugar, and one cup of water. Dissolve the sugar in water and boil this mixture for ten to twelve minutes. Remove from heat and after the solution has cooled for a few minutes add one-half teaspoon of maple flavoring. If you want to get creative, experiment with various kinds of flavorings to produce some of the more exotic kinds of syrup such as are usually found only in specialty pancake restaurants.

14. Get involved in refunding. While cents-off coupons are beneficial, they are nowhere near as profitable as refunding. Here's how refunding works: Occasionally in an effort to introduce a new product or to promote an old one whose sales are lagging, a manufacturer will offer what amounts to a bribe in order to get you to try that product. You buy the item, send him a proof of purchase, and he will send you a refund. Sometimes the refund you get is considerable—up to the entire price of the product. Other times a manufacturer promotes his product by offering a refund for another item which is only indirectly connected with his product. This kind of refund offer falls more into the goodwill area rather than the promotional area. For example, you may see a coupon for chicken on the back of a can of solid vegetable shortening. The manufacturer is offering to reimburse you for buying chicken to fry in his product. You may at first think refunding is not that profitable because you see so few refund offers. But that is not the case at all. Hundreds of refund offers are going on all the time, but the only way you can know about them is by subscribing to a refunding bulletin, which comes out, usually weekly, with a list of all the current refund offers in effect. By working conscientiously at refunding you can make a big cut in your grocery costs, but it takes effort and a certain amount of bookkeeping. If you would like to try refunding, one of the best bulletins is Gold 'n Refunds, Carole Kratz, Editor, Box 262, Hannibal, Ohio 43931. For a sample copy, write to Mrs. Kratz and enclose a stamped, self-addressed envelope so that she can advise you of the current prices.

15. Shop at the most advantageous times. Weekend specials usually start on Thursday. By shopping then you get the jump on the Friday morning shoppers while avoiding the possibility that the store will run out of advertised specials. Shopping early not only helps as far as the specials are concerned but also increases your buying power in other areas. If you wait until Saturday afternoon the stock will be somewhat reduced and you might find it impossible to buy either the size or brand you want. For example, by that time large cans of beans may be sold out and you will have to pay up to 20 percent more by buying two small cans instead.

Sometimes it is all right to be a last minute shopper. If you know of a grocery store that is not open on Sunday, visit it just before closing on Saturday afternoon, and you may find that a large portion of the produce has been marked down. The reason for this is that the produce won't look quite as appealing on Monday and the store wants to clear it out if possible. That, however, does not mean that the produce is inferior. It simply means that the bananas which are ripe on Saturday will be too ripe to sell on Monday. If you can use them right away, you can pick up quite a bargain.

In a similar way you can take advantage of a Sunday closing by buying meats first thing on Monday mornings. The meat left from Saturday will generally be marked down at least one-third. Don't worry about the fact that the meat may have lost some of its bright color. It is still fresh enough. After all, haven't you sometimes kept meat in your own refrigerator for a day or so and then used it even if it had lost some of its fresh color? Steaks and roasts in particular can be good bargains on Monday mornings.

Can We Find Bargains?

Is Bargain Hunting Scriptural?

Bargain hunting for the Christian is more than constantly looking for high value and low price. It is a manifestation of Christian principles. God knows of our needs for food, clothing, and drink (Matt. 6:25-34) and He promises that these needs will be taken care of after the Christian gets his priorities in order. Therefore, since God has promised to provide our food, drink, and clothing, doesn't it represent a lack of trust in Him if we spend money indiscriminately? Bargain hunting can be a witness to our faith in God's ability to provide for us. If five dollars is all we have to spend and the item we need costs twenty dollars, then by refusing to buy what we cannot afford, we are showing our willingness to trust Him to lead us to that which is within our means.

Nearly every Christian I know can recite at least one incidence of how the Lord met a financial need by providing an unexpected bargain. In my life, this has happened so often I have lost count of the number of times it has occurred. For instance, at one time I badly needed new drapes for my bedroom. However, since the windows are oddly shaped and the distance to be covered is about nine feet across, window coverings for that room are quite expensive. It seemed the least I could expect to pay for drapes would be fifty dollars, and that would be only if I found an exceptional bargain. Knowing that I didn't have fifty dollars to spend, I decided to try to get the drapes for about twenty dollars. Accordingly, I began watching newspaper ads and checking the drapery departments of stores where I was shopping for other purchases. Several months passed and still I had no new draperies. But I was determined not to spend more than the twenty dollars I had allotted for that purpose. Then unexpectedly, while shopping for something else I encountered a bargain too good to be true. A pair of draperies in just the right width and length, as well as the right shade of blue, was marked down to a sale price. Eagerly I lifted the price tag, hopefully expecting a sale price of twenty dollars. Instead, the price was six dollars!

Perhaps you are wondering if God is really interested in whether I have bargain-priced draperies for my bedroom. Admittedly, it does seem incredible to think He would intervene in the mundane aspects of our lives. However, since He knows the number of hairs on our heads (Matt. 10:30) and since not even a sparrow dies without His knowledge (Matt. 10:29), it is not at all difficult to believe He will provide for our material needs. Just as Elisha did not hesitate to seek a miracle to retrieve a borrowed ax-head which had fallen into the water (II Kings 6:5-8), neither should we underestimate the providing power of our Lord.

Bargain hunting is not for the purpose of taking care of your own finances instead of allowing the Lord to do it. Rather, when properly used, bargain hunting is the evidence of your faith in God to supply your needs at the price He knows you can afford. Bargain hunting for the Christian should not be a means of gaining money to hoard, but rather a means of showing our faith in God's ability to provide in every aspect of our lives.

"But seek ye first the kingdom of God, and his righteousness; and all these things shall be added unto you" (Matt.

6:33). Just as we, as earthly parents, want what is best for our children, so does God want what is best for His children. "If ye then, being evil, know how to give good gifts unto your children, how much more shall your Father which is in heaven give good things to them that ask him?" (Matt. 7:11).

What Is a Bargain?

While the term *bargain* is a vital word in the vocabulary of the value conscious consumer, a great many shoppers don't seem to know the whole meaning of the word. In reality, price is only one of the criteria to be used in determining a bargain. Here are some of the additional factors necessary for making a sound decision on a product which seems to be a bargain:

1. Do I really need this item? An object is not a bargain at any price if it does not fill a need in your life. Of course, the word *need* may be a bit vague, too. A bargain priced framed picture may be a "need" in your life if the spot over your sofa is bare and if the pleasure to be had in looking at a beautiful scene compensates you for the price. "Need" takes in much more than the essentials of life, because if we get to basics, the only things we truly need are food, water, air, clothing, and shelter. So if a product fills a definite "need" in your life, it may be a bargain even if it is not an "essential."

2. Do I really want this item? While you may desperately need a winter coat, you haven't gotten a bargain if you buy a cheaply priced one that you already hate by the time you get to the cash register. Any item, no matter how inexpensive or well-made it is, is not a bargain if you don't like it. While those living in absolute poverty might be compelled to wear or to use things they dislike, most people have a few more options. If you buy an item you dislike it may never be used, resulting in a need for an item similar to the one just purchased.

3. How long have I wanted the item? If you have been thinking about buying an item for days or even months, it may be something you truly want. However, if the want occurred only after seeing the item at a sale, perhaps you had better exercise caution. Such factors as shopping with a friend, or low prices, or seeing other customers snatching up similar items may be motivating you to get on the bandwagon.

4. Would I want the item if it were not sale priced? Perhaps you have had your heart set on a powder blue cashmere sweater but the one you found on sale is apricot. Is the fact that the apricot sweater costs half as much as the blue the element that makes the sale priced one appealing? While you planned to wear the blue one with nearly every skirt in your wardrobe, will buying the apricot one necessitate buying other things to match it? A bargain is not a bargain if buying it leads to further expense. In the case of clothing it is cheaper in the long run to buy the item that is not on sale if it is the one you really want and the one that fits most readily into your wardrobe.

5. Is this an honest sale price? Some less than scrupulous dealers create so called bargains in an effort to hike sales. Perhaps you find something which catches your eye and the tag reads, "was $99.99, now only $49.99." Is it a bargain? That depends on a number of factors. Have you ever seen the item sold at the higher price? If not, it may be the dealer's ploy to get your attention. (It is rare to find an item on sale for less than half of its true worth, unless it is hopelessly out-of-style clothing.) Even if that particular dealer did originally sell the item for $99.99, are the discount chain stores in your area advertising it for $59.99? If so, then the true savings you will get by buying the $49.99 item is not fifty dollars, but only ten dollars, since with careful shopping you could have had the item for $59.99 without the sale.

6. Is this the best possible price? While a 10 percent reduction in price might look wonderful, you should not grab hastily. If one store has a 10 percent off sale going on, might not another store have a 15 percent off sale at the same time? Even if a price seems good, check around before committing yourself to the first sale you find.

7. Is the quality acceptable? Many people are accustomed to thinking that only the best will do, when at times second best is perfectly acceptable for the purpose you have in mind. For example, in washing machines, each company makes about five different models. The most expensive model does practically everything for you except walk to the clothes hamper and sort the laundry, while the least expensive model simply washes and may not have such options as bleach dispenser, self-cleaning filter, and water temperature variations. While the lowest priced model probably won't be what you had in mind, the top line model may have features you will never use. Somewhere between the deluxe model and the basic model you will probably find your best buy. Wait until the model you want goes on sale instead of buying the top line model on sale and rationalizing that it represents a greater savings. If you buy more quality than you need, you still don't have a bargain.

Clothing purchases represent a real challenge to the bargain conscious consumer who is looking for quality. Should you pay extra to get finished seams and hand-picked zippers? Probably not. Look instead for such things as good fit and quality fabric. You can add a few expensive looking details yourself if you wish.

8. Is this item of lasting quality or is it a fad? Let's suppose you need a pair of shoes and you find a high quality name brand pair drastically reduced. Should you buy them? Look carefully before you decide. No matter how inexpensive the shoes or how well-made, they are not a bargain if you will be ashamed to wear them within three months because of their hopelessly outdated styling. A real bargain retains not only its quality, but its appeal. This is not to imply that every item you buy must be so classic as to still be in style in ten years, but rather that every item should not become outdated before you have received your money's worth in wear.

9. Can I afford it? While it might seem at first that any bargain should be snatched up quickly lest it be missed, that is not the case at all. No matter how many of the other criteria a product meets, if you can't afford it, you haven't found a true bargain. Any bargain which creates a financial strain and tension isn't worthwhile.

10. Can I afford to maintain it? Some things may pass all other tests but fail the final test of a true bargain. Some purchases eventually cost far more than the price paid in the store. For instance, let's suppose you see a white skirt of exceptional quality at an affordable price. You need a new white skirt and you really want one made just as this one is made. Is it a bargain? Look a little further. Does it have a "dry clean only" tag? If so, you may find that the slightly higher priced washable skirt on another rack may, in the long run, be the better buy.

The factor of maintenance and operational cost applies to a great many things. A room-size air conditioner doesn't cost much, but over a period of years the cost of the electricity to run it is quite expensive. The free poodle your neighbor wants to give you looks like a real bargain, too, but have you considered food, veterinarian visits, and twice-monthly grooming? Perhaps you have just about convinced yourself to buy a new car and figure you can buy an economy model and then compensate for the payments by cutting down on gas consumption. But have you calculated higher insurance premiums on a late model car? How about higher license plate fees? Will the higher maintenance costs of a foreign car destroy any savings created by the use of less gasoline?

Becoming Aware of Savings Possibilities

Virtually, every woman thinks of herself as a bargain hunter, but few people really are. The difference between the person who thinks she is a bargain hunter and the person who genuinely is one is largely a matter of awareness and planning. Here are some of the ways she achieves awareness:

1. She reads the ads. Most shoppers glance through the newspaper ads only when they plan to make a major purchase, but the true bargain hunter studies the ads even when she is not buying. She learns the approximate prices of many products and files these figures away in her mind for future reference.

2. She talks to her friends. There was a time when it was considered extremely poor manners to discuss money matters with anyone except your own family, but today's economic situation now makes it imperative that we help each other as much as possible. Certainly your friend has a right to be offended if you bluntly ask how much she paid for her new dress or sofa, but most likely she won't mind at all if you initiate a conversation about the most economical place to buy groceries, toiletries or school supplies. Since you probably can't cover all the stores in town, it is a big help to solicit your friends' opinions on places they have shopped.

3. She and her friends shop cooperatively. Before two of my friends took jobs, which gave them less time to bargain hunt, the three of us had a cooperative shopping system. Since we live in three different suburbs each of us shops in different stores. If I wanted a bargain priced long-sleeved white shirt for my husband, I would enlist my friends' aid in searching for a bargain. If either of them spotted a good deal they telephoned me. I also did the same for them.

4. She works from a "want" list. The true bargain hunter has a definite game plan. She knows her wants and needs and doesn't let the stores plan her shopping for her. By knowing her family's needs in advance, she can plan her shopping at the most advantageous times. When she does spot a good price on a needed item she knows immediately if it fits in her budget.

5. She knows the alternatives. The conscientious bargain hunter has all the facts. She knows whether a purchased dress is a better bargain than a home-sewn one because she knows approximately what the home-sewn one represents in both cost and time. She also shops at manufacturer's outlets, second-hand shops, and garage sales.

6. She has flexibility. The bargain hunter must know how, on a moment's notice, to accurately evaluate a potential bargain's place in her schedule of buying. She must have an inventory of goods already on hand in order to know if a change in buying plans will work. For example, suppose she does not have chicken written on her shopping list but discovers an unadvertised special on chicken. By knowing the inventory of her pantry, she can quickly decide whether switching from the beef dishes she had planned to chicken dishes will be practical. By knowing that she has no sage or noodles, she may opt for passing up the less expensive chicken, because she would have to buy more "fixings" to go with it.

Likewise, if she has planned to buy a brown skirt and finds a dark blue one on sale instead, she can quickly evaluate her wardrobe and determine that the blue one would work just as well with her white blouse. Flexibility is a must for a bargain hunter.

Store Promotions

Before anyone can become a proficient bargain hunter she must accept one fact: stores are in business to make money and *only* to make money. Every promotion is designed for that purpose. A smart shopper knows how to let a sale work for her rather than for the store. Here's how that is done:

1. Know the actual price of the sale item. Forget all about the "manufacturer's suggested list price"; that figure is largely a myth. Instead, find out the rock bottom price a product is being sold for in the lowest overhead sales operation in town. Check with manufacturer's outlets and catalog showrooms. A $200 item marked down to $125 by the largest department store in town is still not a bargain if you can get it every day of the week for $120 at the somewhat disorganized and occasionally dusty outlet store in your neighborhood.

2. *Know the limitations.* Know if a product requires additional purchases in order for the sale price to be valid or if no returns are allowed on sale items before driving all the way across town in pursuit of a bargain. Also check to see if the sale items are limited warranty merchandise or demonstrator merchandise offered "as is." And know if only a limited number of items can be purchased at the sale price. While it might be worthwhile to drive five miles to save 50 percent on a whole case of shampoo or lotion, it isn't worthwhile to drive that far if only "one per customer" is allowed.

3. *Plan ahead.* Often when truly spectacular savings are offered, particularly on expensive items such as appliances, a crowd of other shoppers will be competing with you. If you suspect this may happen, visit the store before the sale. Learn the layout of the store so you can go directly to the sale area on the day of the sale. Ask the salesman to demonstrate the item for you or to answer any questions you may have on the day before the sale. By doing all these things the day before, you can go directly to the item on sale and, without wasting time on demonstrations and conversations, can quickly make your purchase. You should plan ahead particularly if the item on sale is offered in limited quantities.

4. *Arrive early.* The bargain hunter's best friend may be her alarm clock. It isn't possible to get the same buys in the afternoon as in the morning. The serious shopper should be positioned at the door well in advance of the announced opening time. If the sale is a spectacular one, arrive as much as a half hour in advance in order to position yourself near the door when the opening rush starts.

5. *Learn to speak "store."* Do you know the meanings of such terms as *loss leaders*, *demos*, and *catalog returns*? If not,

learn to speak the same language as the store owners in order to get the best bargains.

A *loss leader* is an item the store sells near or below the wholesale price. Stores use loss leaders to boost other sales. The grocery store which sells sugar or coffee or mayonnaise at a price too good to resist is going to get a great deal of extra business. Bargain shoppers will buy the loss leaders and leave, but most shoppers rationalize, "While I'm here I might as well buy the rest of my groceries," and thus fall into the trap set by the use of the loss leaders.

Demos is short for demonstration models. Often good value can be found in these cars and appliances, since the warranty on them will usually be the same as the one on a new item. Before you buy, however, get that guarantee in writing. The guarantee should start the day you buy the demo, not the day the dealer started using it.

Floor models are similar to demos, except that they actually have not been used except as part of a display.

Sample or *model* items, particularly garments, are those which have been used to demonstrate a particular line to the store's buyers. Garment manufacturers put on fashion shows for retailers—one way store buyers select the garments. After the manufacturer's designer completes his sketch, a model garment, usually in a small size such as an eight or ten, is made to be displayed to prospective buyers. If the design is approved the style goes into production. If not, the design is scrapped. Buying a sample or model garment may, or may not, mean you are getting a one-of-a-kind dress.

Catalog returns are those items brought back to stores such as Sears, Penneys, or Wards by customers who ordered the merchandise through the catalog. You won't see these items in regular retail stores, but they are popular in outlet stores.

Manufacturer's rebate is the name given to a refund which is given to the customer, not by the store but by the product maker. Usually the manufacturer's rebate has nothing to do with the price charged by the store, although in some cases the store emphasizes the rebate as part of its sales promotion for the product. Most of the time the rebate is given through the mail after you have sent in the appropriate cash register tape and product code.

Buying out of Season

One of the most effective means of cutting costs is by buying out of season. Probably every shopper has used this technique at one time or another, but are you using it to maximum advantage? Of course you know that Christmas goods are half price on December 26, sheets are on sale in January, and summer clothing is marked down after the Fourth of July, but do you know the most advantageous time for buying insulation for your attic or tires for your car?

To determine the best time to get good prices on the things you need, try to see prices through the eyes of the seller. Would you, if you were the seller, put tires on sale in June, July, and August when people are going on vacation, or would you wait until a time when sales are down? The same principle is true for any product you want to buy. It isn't going to be on sale during the time of peak demand. Sale prices are engineered for getting customers into stores during times when they are taking their dollars elsewhere.

Especially good out-of-season bargains are to be had on items which must be installed. Large companies have payrolls to be met fifty-two weeks a year and slack periods of business hurt greatly. That is why the air conditioning contractor can give you such a good price in November and December. His men have little to do at that time and he would rather cut prices and have them do something for their paycheck. Similarly, summertime is a good time to have insulation put in your attic, autumn is a good time to add a patio, and the spring months are a good time to add a fireplace.

September and December are the worst months for buying clothing. Anything that could be used as a Christmas gift will not be on sale during December, and this includes everything from dishwashers and color televisions to automobiles. However, some stores do try to entice you with loss leaders on such things as men's shirts or even countertop appliances in December, so this month cannot be written off as a total shopping loss.

January white sales have traditionally been the bargain hunter's peak time for stocking up on linens. An analysis of this sale shows you the kind of thinking which prompts most sales. When do linens sell best? They sell well in spring months because of the great number of June weddings. When do linens sell the slowest? They probably don't move at all immediately after Christmas because by then most shoppers are short of cash. The solution? Put the linens on sale in January!

Another out-of-season advantage can be had in buying discontinued styles. Everybody knows that dress lengths and designs change, but did you know that linen fashions fluctuate, too? Flowers and stripes may continue year after year, but bedspreads with football heroes on them and towels with cartoon characters emblazoned across them wax and wane in popularity. Bold colors become the going thing only to give way to delicate pastels. Therefore, if you buy only what you like, you can find a large savings in buying discontinued styles.

Car buyers have long known the dollar advantage in buying a car at the end of a model change, but did you know that appliances have yearly model changes too?

Other Kinds of Stores

If you have the idea that the only place worth shopping is your neighborhood shopping mall, you will need to revise your opinion if you are serious about becoming an effective bargain hunter. Here are just a few of the other options you have:

1. Surplus stores sell goods which somebody—either the United States Army and Navy or the local department store—bought in excess. As a result there is too much of a particular item in inventory and it must be cleared out. Surplus stores usually offer good prices but not the best selection. One has to shop to see what is available. A great many of the products offered may not be just what you had in mind, because, in some instances, particularly in surplus stores run by large department store chains, the surplus merchandise is the retail buyer's mistake. He may have thought green plaid pajamas were going to be big sellers, but they were not and as a consequence wound up as surplus. Some items get into the surplus store because they originally carried a price tag too high to make them appealing. Once the price is cut in half many more customers are interested. Other surplus store items are there because of their popularity. When an item sells like hotcakes, it may be that only one or two are left at the end of a season, and, rather than carry them on inventory, the store manager sends them to the surplus store.

2. *Sample stores* sell clothing which manufacturers have used to show to prospective wholesale buyers. Generally sample clothing is made up in smaller sizes, such as six, eight, and ten.

3. *"No frills" warehouses* are becoming popular, particularly in the grocery industry. Large savings can be had in these "do-it-yourself" stores. In order to cut costs the store offers no grocery sacks, no bag boys, and no carryout service. Groceries are not even stacked on shelves. Instead, tops are cut off cartons and you take what you want directly out of the box. If you want a sack to put your groceries in, you bring your own and, of course, you do your own bagging. In most of these stores prices are not stamped on each can or box. Instead, you are given a printed list of prices as you enter the store. Although you can find some name brand items, most products are house brands which offer a savings of up to 50 percent over name brands.

Warehouse grocery stores carry no perishable items such as meats or vegetables, so shopping there will mean an extra stop for you.

4. Bulk suppliers. These stores work similar to the warehouse stores except that limits are set on what you buy. Instead of buying one bottle of inexpensive ketchup, you must buy a whole case in order to take advantage of the sale. The disadvantages of this kind of operation are obvious. Most of us don't have the storage space for cases of goods. However, if you do have the room, or if you have an exceptionally large family, these stores do offer some especially good bargains. Another way of taking advantage of these savings is to find one or two friends willing to split a case of goods with you so that all of you may take advantage of the savings without having to cope with storage problems.

Bulk supplier stores generally don't advertise so you will have to scout around to find them.

5. Manufacturer's outlets are operated by the same company who makes the goods. Frequently the surroundings in which you will shop are dreary, and in many cases dressing rooms are not available, but the prices are good. Most of the labels will be cut out, but it doesn't take a great deal of intelligence to discern that most of what is being sold was made on the other side of the store wall where sewing machines are busily humming away.

6. Retail outlets differ from manufacturers' outlets in that numerous brands are offered for sale. The seller does not necessarily make the items offered. Rather, he buys discontinued styles, sample dresses, and surplus stock from various companies. Again, you will find the labels have been cut out, but the store owner is usually clever enough to leave a few pertinent letters on the tag in order for you to figure out the original label.

How to Become an Educated Buyer

Do you know how to cut up your own chickens? Do you know what bulb wattage works best in your living room lamp? Do you know how to use a humidifier to cut energy costs? Knowing such things can help you in your bargain hunting.

The educated buyer goes shopping with a head full of facts and usable ideas. She is smart, inventive, and knows her field. As a result, she is the one who finds the most bargains. Here are a few of the ways bargain hunting ability can be increased:

1. Know your field. If you took up skydiving you would probably read books on theory and how-to before ever making that first leap. Bargain hunters need this kind of study for their field also. Failure to learn is one of the greatest hindrances to the development of bargain hunting ability. Before attempting to transform yourself into a bargain hunter read everything possible on the subject. Go to the public library and ask the librarian for help. He will show you books on nutrition, home decorating, sewing, appliance repair, grocery shopping, cleaning, and much much more. If that doesn't answer most of your questions contact the United States Printing Office. The superintendent of documents has booklets on virtually every subject.

2. Never stop learning. The bargain hunter who thinks she knows all there is to know about comparison shopping is missing a great deal. The bargain hunting techniques that worked well for your mother and grandmother may not apply anymore. With new products bombarding the marketplace, no one can be knowledgeable about everything.

3. Learn from past mistakes. It is less of a disaster to forget the name of the brand of tuna that you really loved than it is to forget the name of the brand you hated. Make a note, either mental or written, of brands that do not add up to your expectations. Don't make the mistake of buying them again.

4. Educate the manufacturers. If a product doesn't perform properly, let the manufacturer know about it. He wants to please consumers and will appreciate your comments. Write a polite letter briefly stating why you did not like the product. He may send you a refund or a coupon for a free product from one of his other lines. Likewise, if a product is especially good, let him know that. Expression of your approval may bring you a discount coupon.

5. ***Understand the terminology.*** Do you know the difference between percale and muslin? Between first-cut and center-cut pork chops? Such information is necessary for intelligent comparison shopping. If you see terms you don't recognize ask a store clerk, your mother, your neighbor, or even another customer what the unfamiliar terms mean. If all else fails head for the library and do research on the terminology that puzzles you.

Can We Beat Inflation?

More Money and Higher Prices

It's a familiar story: as soon as you get a raise prices go up. The result is that even though you have more money you have less buying power. This is enough to discourage even the most conscientious bargain hunter.

The major villain is inflation. Today's dollar is not worth what it was worth in 1930 or even in 1970. The price of goods must increase as the value of the dollar decreases. That is why more and more dollars are needed to purchase the goods you require.

If it is any consolation, our country is not the only one suffering from this monetary problem. Some countries are now faced with inflation rates as high as 60 percent. To cope with the problem larger denominations of currency are being issued and smaller bills are being phased out. Our own problems may seem bothersome to us, but we can be thankful that our own economic woes have not reached this proportion.

Many factors cause inflation, making it difficult to control. Much of the inflation problem lies in situations beyond the understanding of the average person, but some blame comes back to the average American. Increased wages, the demand for things formerly considered luxuries, the lack of interest in savings, and the abuse of credit are all contributing factors which feed inflation.

Rising costs are not a new problem. II Kings 6:25 tells of a time during Elisha's day when "an ass's head was sold for fourscore pieces of silver, and the fourth part of a cab of dove's dung for five pieces of silver." At that time Samaria was under seige and the people were starving to death. The economic laws of supply and demand worked then as they do now; when food was low in supply and greatly in demand the prices rose. Later, because of a miracle in which the Lord frightened away the enemy, food became plentiful again and the prices fell: "So a measure of fine flour was sold for a shekel, and two measures of barley for a shekel, according to the word of the Lord" (II Kings 7:16b).

Just as the laws of supply and demand made the price of goods fluctuate in Elisha's day, so it does in ours. Inflation is one of the prices paid for the high standard of living we enjoy. As more people obtain more money more goods are available, thus requiring more money, which in turn requires higher wages, which in turn sends prices upward.

Another inflation factor is that labor has become expensive and few of us are "do-it-yourselfers." Your father or grandfather may have repaired the kitchen sink, put up the storm windows, and mowed the lawn themselves, but today many of us hire workers to do these jobs. Since people put increasingly higher price tags on the value of their services, every job we fail to do for ourselves costs us a great deal.

Inflation and You

What does all this talk about inflation have to do with you? Perhaps you are not interested in politics or economics and can see no real reason to concern yourself with the whys and wherefores of inflation. All you are interested in is better living.

Understanding inflation can help you live better. By learning how it affects your wallet and your lifestyle you equip yourself to give inflation a good bruising even if you are unable to give it an actual beating.

We cannot reverse rising oil prices or increase dwindling oil supplies, but we can participate in measures designed to cut back on oil needs. We cannot turn a credit happy society around by ourselves, but we can exercise the kind of good stewardship which shows the world a difference in our lives. We cannot singlehandedly control the rise in prices, but we can exercise self-control by refusing to buy outrageously priced items.

Decreased Consumption

Two messages to the manufacturers of the products we use daily can do more than anything else to change the prices of those products: "Give us more!" sends the price up, while "We don't want any!" sends the price plummeting. Try pricing Christmas trees on December 26 if you don't believe this.

One effective way consumers can send out a plea for lower prices is by refusing to buy products which are overpriced. This is what happened a few years ago when bad weather ruined a large portion of the sugar cane crop and sent the price of sugar to unbelievable heights. Within a few months the price of sugar doubled. Soon it doubled again, resulting in consumers drastically cutting back on their purchases of sugar. Eventually a new crop of sugar cane came in and prices went down.

Rising oil prices are a problem for most of us. Repeatedly the government has issued bulletins advising us that only by cutting consumption can we hope to ever get those prices down, but we continue taking Sunday drives and we continue keeping our houses too warm.

Take a stand against inflation by cutting back or by eliminating those products which cost more than they should. Cut back on your driving. Turn your thermostat down. Find substitutes for overpriced foods. Learn to be a do-it-yourselfer. Be a conscientious bargain hunter.

Credit and Its Role in Inflation

Do you have a credit card? If not, you are a member of an unusual minority group—those who pay cash instead of charging their purchases. While many people do use their credit cards wisely and get into no financial trouble, millions more cannot resist the temptation of overspending. Overuse of credit fuels the flame of inflation.

Perhaps you disagree with me about the problems of credit, so I will challenge you to a test. Even if you have never had credit problems, try putting away your credit cards for three months and go on a cash-only basis. Quite likely, you will discover that the act of pulling money out of your wallet has a restraining influence on your buying habits.

Admittedly, most of us could never have a home of our own or even a car without the use of credit, but for most families this is not a real problem. The difficulties come when credit is used to finance luxuries or day-to-day expenses such as toothpaste and gasoline.

Credit fosters both the love of money and the love of things. By making it easy for the Christian woman to have things before she has disciplined herself to save up sufficient funds, credit causes an unhealthy desire for money. This, then, is the first step toward the love that has no place in a Christian's life: "For the love of money is the root of all evil; which while some coveted after, they have erred from the faith, and pierced themselves through with many sorrows" (I Tim. 6:10).

Predictably, credit problems seem to intensify during times of inflation. In spite of the heavy percentage rates charged for the privilege of having credit, many consumers reason that it is still cheaper to buy on credit rather than to wait until they have sufficient cash funds. Most buyers think if they wait until they can afford the item they want that item will cost more. By buying today on credit, they believe they are getting a better bargain. This is the theory of "paying yesterday's debts with tomorrow's less valuable dollars." While on large items such as houses and cars, which must be financed for years rather than months, this idea does have a certain amount of validity, it isn't true with purchases of lower priced items. It leads the shopper to buy more than she needs because she becomes conditioned to buying things she *may* need in the future rather than waiting to see if the need is a genuine one.

The abuse of credit is one of the contributing factors in the continuing cycle of inflation. As inflation makes the use of credit more attractive, an endless circle develops. Unbelievable as it may seem, credit is used more during times of *apparent* prosperity than during times when families are in tight financial circumstances because of emergencies.

Much of the problem with credit buying comes from the lack of education today's consumers have concerning credit. While those who lived through the Depression had an opportunity to learn firsthand the economic facts of life, those of us who were born after that time have been raised in a different manner. While your grandparents may have looked with horror on purchasing goods on credit, successive generations have felt no such qualms. The credit industry has convinced many that being in debt is a status symbol and not a problem. Even the terminology is wrong: *credit*, as it was originally used in bookkeeping, meant adding on or a plus figure, not an amount owed. The real name for credit cards should be "debt cards" but since no one would want a thing like that, the card issuing corporations have used a bit of psychology and have, with the use of a positive sounding word, created a new image for their operations.

Inflation and Savings

With inflation chomping away at your savings acount faster than you can accumulate funds, you may ask yourself if it is really worthwhile to put money in a savings account. The idea of saving is still a good one, but a savings account is not always the best way to save.

Everybody needs three kinds of savings: 1) savings for specific purposes, such as a new washing machine or braces for a child's teeth; 2) savings for times when either income or expenses are changed drastically (commonly called the "rainy day" fund); 3) savings for long-term goals such as retirement.

Savings, however, are not to take the place of dependence on God's provision. There is nothing wrong with putting away a few months' salary for a time when it might be needed for emergencies, but the rainy day fund should not lead a Christian into hoarding. Prudence is commendable, but greed is the basis for hoarding and under no circumstances a Christian attribute.

While the wealthy invest in such things as gold and silver and certain kinds of stocks which are somewhat inflation resistant, the majority of us must look for more traditional ways to invest our savings. Two ways of making more interest are by opening an account in a savings and loan institution or credit union and by purchasing short-term savings certificates. However, these savings certificates tie up an investor's money for one to three years.

The reason savings and loan associations and credit unions pay more interest than banks is because by putting your funds into one of these institutions you are actually becoming an investor in the corporation itself. This is why the interest rates there fluctuate more than the interest rates in banks. Current interest rates depend to a certain extent on the institution's current overall earnings.

With all the drawbacks involved in trying to deal with inflation, does it actually pay for the Christian to open a savings account? Definitely so! The interest that you receive is in no way the whole picture of the worth of your savings account.

Savings accounts not only offer you a means of financial discipline, but also help you to avoid the use of credit. When used as a means of avoiding interest rates of 18 to 24 percent, the savings account takes on new significance. If it takes you a year to save for a new washing machine, the price will go up, but it is highly unlikely it will go up enough to offset the interest rate you would have paid by buying it on credit.

Inflation and Moonlighting

Look around at the lifestyles of your friends. You probably know at least two or three families where the husband holds a moonlighting job. More and more people are now finding it necessary to work two jobs. For some, the extra income is not even "gravy" but a means of trying to meet current expenses.

Like the circle of credit and inflation, extra money and inflation form another alliance. As consumers get extra money, they demand more goods. More goods mean more workers who also want higher wages. Then the price of the goods goes up. Because everybody has more money the demand remains constant. Eventually the circle comes back to its starting point and the result is the same: the more money one has, the more he wants. This situation is not a new one. About a thousand years before Christ the writer of Ecclesiastes observed, "He that loveth silver shall not be satisfied with silver; nor he that loveth abundance with increase: this is also vanity" (Eccles. 5:10).

It might look as if taking a second job would be the answer to a family's financial problems, but often this is not the case. If sudden and monumental expenses, such as doctor bills, make it necessary for the husband to take on a second job, this may work out, but if the moonlight job is strictly for the purpose of buying more things, the job is contributing to inflation.

The sad thing is that most men who do take on moonlight jobs find it impossible to ever give them up. First they intend to work only until certain debts are paid. Then they decide to buy something on installment while the extra money is coming in. Eventually the family upgrades its standard of living and the husband finds himself working two jobs just to make ends meet.

A less disastrous method would be to fight inflation by cutting back on goods and services. Learn to buy everything at the best possible time and price and train yourself to be a do-it-yourselfer. These are the only intelligent ways to cope with the problem. Moonlighting may help in the short run, but eventually it is going to cause more problems than it cures.

The Vacation Vacuum

"Come . . . and Rest Awhile . . ."

The word *vacation* means a time of rest, but for most of us it is anything but restful. Clothing must be purchased and packed, car repairs made, traveler's checks bought, and afterwards, charge account bills paid.

Yet a vacation is one of the best ideas ever to come to the working world. People need time off from their regular activities to recharge themselves.

Jesus recognized the need for a period of time away from the routine of daily work. While His work was of immense importance, He knew that the physical bodies of He and His disciples could not take the pace of constant work and no relaxation. After a particularly difficult time for the apostles Jesus "said unto them, Come ye yourselves apart into a desert place, and rest a while: for there were many coming and going, and they had no leisure so much as to eat" (Mark 6:31).

A vacation, in the truest sense of the word, is not a period of hustle and bustle, but rather a time of physical rest and mental reflection. While traveling and engaging in recreational activities may be a means of attaining some of the mental and physical rest needed, a real vacation is one which leaves the family relaxed and with a good attitude.

But marriage counselors point out that the two-week vacation period is one of the most dangerous times of the year as far as marital harmony is concerned. For some reason, most marriages cannot bear the strain of two solid weeks of unrelieved togetherness. Vacation time frequently turns into a time of battle with parents squabbling and children sulking.

Financial counselors suspect that financial strain is another reason for vacation upsets. Incredible as it may seem, those families who are the most deeply in debt are the ones who may be vacationing the most often and in the most expensive manner. The vacation is rationalized on the basis of "Let's get away for a while and forget our money worries."

If you are trying to run from money worries, the hundreds of dollars you may spend will not bring happiness. The best way to get the most value for your vacation dollar is to plan your vacation with worthwhile motives in mind.

What Shall We Do on Vacation?

The kinds of vacations available to you are as varied as the seashells you collected on the beach last summer. You can take a sports oriented vacation with a concentration of golf or tennis, a back-to-nature vacation with the emphasis on hiking, horseback riding, and camping, or a rest-and-recharge vacation with beautiful scenery and little to do, or even a remodeling vacation during which you paint your house. The choice is yours, but the presence or absence of money should not be the determining factor, because with careful planning you will be able to achieve the results you want, even on a limited budget.

With ample funds you can go to an exotic island and golf on a secluded course, however, if your funds aren't so ample you can still accomplish your goal. The difference is you will be staying at home and playing golf on the public course. Whatever the current shape of your budget, the kind of vacation you want to enjoy is possible provided you are able to be flexible in your choice of location.

The best way to get the most vacation value for your dollar is to select the kind of vacation that pleases you and to scale it up or down to fit your budget.

If fishing is what you want to do, then by all means do it, but you don't have to do it in South America. With the exception of oceanside or skiing vacations, any activity you might choose is probably available to you on either a local level or only a day's drive away.

What Shall We Wear?

Second in importance only to "Where shall we go?" is "What shall we wear?" Other than Christmas and back-to-school time, the period of time preceeding a vacation probably accounts for more clothing purchases than any other time of the year.

In order to economize it is necessary to pinpoint both your destination and your lifestyle. If you decide to undertake something new, such as skiing, you may find yourself investing more in clothing and equipment than in the actual vacation. Therefore, when planning a vacation which involves some activity you have not participated in previously, take into consideration the cost of the clothing and equipment involved as well as the expenses of the vacation itself.

Most shoppers who buy new clothing for vacation make two major mistakes: they buy too much or they buy the wrong items. The first place you will need to go shopping when you are planning your vacation, is in your own closet. Look to see what useable outfits you already own, and plan your purchases around them. Everybody likes new things to wear on vacation, but cutting down on vacation clothing is one of the most effective means of holding down the cost of a vacation.

If possible, plan your vacation clothing purchases the previous year. Admittedly, children's wear will have to be purchased at the time of the vacation, but items for the adult members of the family can be purchased advantageously at the end-of-summer sales. Such things as jeans, casual knit shirts, sandals, underclothing, straw purses, and separates, such as skirts and blouses, are not going to change styles much between the August purchase date and next year's June vacation.

Looking Ahead

It is a good idea to start preparing for your next vacation as soon as you return from this one. How is this done? First, learn to be alert for sales on items you will need for vacation, regardless of where you go. Such things as toothpaste, toiletries, sunglasses, first aid supplies, tanning lotion, stamps, maps, and even film for your camera can be bought up to a year in advance. (When you buy film ahead of time, do what professional photographers do to keep film fresh. Put it in a plastic freezer container that seals snugly and store it in your refrigerator.)

Basically, the miscellaneous items which must go along with you will be the same whether you hike in the Rockies or scuba dive in the Caribbean. That's why you can save so much money by stocking up before vacation time. I like to buy one or two items each week until I have completed my vacation list. Then as the box of bandages or the bottle of shampoo is purchased, it can go directly into the small cosmetics case that is part of my luggage. By the time vacation season arrives I don't have to worry about getting all this together, because it is already packed.

If you like to take along some reading material, this, too, can be gathered in advance. Take in a few garage sales and accumulate some low-cost reading matter. Games for the children can be bought after Christmas. However, it is best to be a bit secretive about these purchases. Let the new coloring book and crayons be a surprise until you pass them out in the car after a few hours of driving. Other good playthings are simple games without multiple pieces, tiny dolls, a jar of bubble liquid for entertainment during rest stops, pencils and paper for recording such things as how many Iowa license plates are spotted or how many brown cows are on which side of the road, and small individual maps so the children can plot the course of the trip for themselves instead of asking you every five minutes.

If you have to take any medicine on a regular basis, buy that in advance also. There is nothing like being five hundred miles from home and discovering that you have left your asthma prescription at home. If you are prone to ailments requiring aspirin, antacids, or decongestants take these along with you, too. Your corner pharmacy sells these items much more cheaply than does the specialty shop in the hotel lobby.

What Kind of Transportation?

One of the major expenses involved with a vacation is the matter of getting there. Let's look at some of the options available to you in the transportation department.

1. By car. For most of us the favored method of vacation travel is by family car. Even with the cost of gasoline rising almost daily, it is still cheaper to go by car if you have to transport a group to your destination.

How then can we get the most economy for the family vehicle? First, before ever pulling out of the driveway, make certain the car is in tiptop running shape. Are the brakes sound and the battery reliable? Do such things as windshield wipers, headlights, taillights, and turn signals work effectively? Do you have a jack and a useable spare tire? Is the car free of mechanical defects? Are the tires free of signs of excessive wear?

The best way to avoid financial disaster on a trip is to take care of all known automotive problems before you go. Should you have to spend one day of your vacation standing around a greasy garage, you will know how important preventive maintenance really is. Not only will you likely pay an exorbitant price for the repairs you will need, you will also pay the price of having missed a day's entertainment or relaxation.

On some interstate highways there has been a great deal of fraud perpetrated on vacationers by unscrupulous service station operators. While most states are cracking down on these notorious operations, some still exist. Don't leave your car unattended at a service station. Doing so means that you may get charged for more gasoline or oil than you actually bought. It also gives these con artists a chance to puncture your radiator hose or slit your fan belt so they can sell you a new one.

Increasing gasoline mileage is an important means of cutting vacation costs and three ways of boosting gasoline mileage can be done by any traveler: 1) Before you go on vacation have your car tuned up and have new spark plugs and a new air filter installed. These measures can increase gasoline mileage significantly. Also, have the oil changed. This doesn't affect the gasoline mileage, but it does prevent some other costly problems. 2) Don't overload your car. Not only does too much weight cost you in terms of tires and shock absorbers, but it also decreases your gasoline efficiency. 3) Drive the speed limit and maintain a smooth, even pace. Starting and stopping quickly burns up extra gasoline, and driving too fast not only leaves you open for a speeding ticket but increases your car's consumption of fuel.

Good tires are vital to your family's safety. Therefore the purchase of new tires may be an integral part of your vacation expense. Since you know in advance that vacation season is coming, make it a point to purchase the best tires you can afford during the months they are on sale. Plan ahead in order to get the best prices. You won't find the same bargains in June, July, and August as you will in March and April. After buying those tires keep them inflated with the proper amount of air pressure to increase both the life of the tires and your gas mileage. You will also get a smoother ride.

2. ***By plane.*** Now that gasoline for the family car has become so expensive, many people, even those who previously never thought of flying, are now wondering if it is possible to save money by traveling by air rather than car. If only one person is going and special discount rates can be utilized, air fare may offer a savings. However, if the entire family is going along, air travel is still more expensive than is travel in the family car. But when the difference in time of travel is considered, the price gap might not seem so great. Traveling long distances by car makes it necessary to pay for several day's lodgings and meals. Air travel offers the advantage of getting to your destination in hours rather than in days. On the negative side, however, there is the matter of transportation once you reach your destination. The price of a rental car or taxis must be taken into consideration when comparing prices. Airline fares range from full-price, first-class daytime rates to standby half-price rates. Somewhere in between these two extremes lies your best travel bargain.

As a rule, night fares are cheaper than day fares, tourist accommodations are cheaper than first-class accommodations, and excursion rates are cheaper than simply going and coming any time you wish. To get the cheapest rates, inquire first about the nighttime, tourist-rate, excursion tickets. "Nighttime" usually means the hours after 9:00 p.m. and before 8:00 a.m. "Tourist" means a slight change in seating position and a variation in menu. "Excursion" means that when you buy your round-trip ticket you arrange to use the return ticket at a time convenient for the airline. Excursion rates are available from some airlines if you are gone at least a week. Others ask for a ten-day or two-week interval in flights. To further cut costs, ask about off-season rates or special cost cuts available if you agree to fly during a slack period such as the middle of the week.

Other special discounts add to the savings and to the confusion. In some instances, if the whole family is going, the mother and children may fly for half price. The age of the children makes a difference in some instances, so mention this when you book. Vacationers over the age of sixty-five get additional discounts.

If you are traveling alone and are not in a hurry, consider using the standby system. You pay about half as much for your ticket and then wait at the airport until a flight is available for you. Often the first plane going to your destination will be less than full.

Since airline fares are so varied and so confusing, check the schedules and rates of several airlines. With tickets costing as much as they do, you will want to be an especially diligent bargain hunter.

3. By train. While train service has continued to grow in popularity in other countries, the United States does not have the kind of train service which makes traveling by rail economical. To operate profitably, railroad lines have had to concentrate on freight carrying instead of passenger service. For this reason, passenger service may not be available in the area you wish to reach.

Train fares are not inexpensive either. Generally, they fall somewhere between the cost of an airplane ticket and the cost of a bus ticket, but since the rail routes are not always direct, bus travel may get you to your destination faster.

Train service is not for the bargain hunter, but if your children have never ridden a train or if you love the feel of the rails, then perhaps the train trip will be enjoyable enough for you to offset the lack of a bargain in cost.

4. By bus. Anyone who has not ridden a bus in a number of years may be surprised at the changes. In order to compete with other forms of transportation most bus lines have initiated various savings plans enabling riders to travel economically.

Like the airlines, the bus lines have devised numerous ways of appealing to bargain hunters. It is possible to buy tickets for unlimited mileage and tour the entire country by simply changing buses whenever you feel like it—all for one fee. Bus service is usually cheaper on weekdays than on weekends. If the entire family is going, that usually entitles you to some sort of discount, too. In addition, there are sometimes special promotions which cut fares even further.

Where Shall We Stay?

Accommodations for vacationers range from tents in National Parks to palatial villas overlooking secluded beaches, but for most of us the options fall somewhere between these two extremes. Basically, your options are taking your shelter with you (tent, mobile home, or camper); staying in a motel or motor inn (usually located near the interstates and the tourist attractions); staying in a hotel (usually located in the center of town or near airports); renting a cottage (generally located in areas with such features as beaches or mountains); or staying in a tourist home (the home of a family who accepts paying guests). Here are some major differences in the various kinds of vacation lodgings:

1. Taking your own. If you enjoy camping—and that term is used loosely today since living in a forty-foot air-conditioned travel trailer can hardly be called roughing it—you should already be aware of such things as travel clubs and directories of roadside camping areas.

One way to get more enjoyment out of your traveling is by being a part of a travel club. These groups often travel as a caravan. Traveling as part of a group means you will have the advantage of not being alone in a strange city, but it also means you may be somewhat limited in your activities. However, the caravan trips are optional, so even if you never go on a trip with the rest of the members, you can still benefit from the club approach. Many clubs print monthly newsletters and with any group of fellow travelers you have the advantage of getting the real story on any destination you choose. No travel brochure can compare with getting firsthand information directly from someone who has been there.

If you are going to "camp" in the most economical manner, you will need to acquire a campground directory. If you have found a chain you like, ask if they have a guide book. Most of them do, and usually the book is free for the asking.

If you are willing to try different chains you will need a comprehensive directory. Most bookstores carry these for under five dollars. In these books nearly every campground in the United States is listed, whether it is part of a chain or a single operation run by one family. These guide books are quite informative, and if you do a great deal of this type of traveling, the books are well worth the price. Each listing gives you not only the price of the accommodations but a run down of the facilities available as well as information on the nearness of tourist spots.

While most buyers rationalize the purchase of a camper as a means of saving money, owning a camper is usually not economical. In reality, a camper is more of a convenience than a bargain. Certainly if you use it twenty years, travel constantly, or make it into a home, a camper is going to be a worthwhile investment financially, but otherwise it probably is not. However, if you already have a camper the expense is behind you, so make it a point to utilize the equipment as much as possible.

2. ***Staying in a motel or motor inn.*** Motels are the end result of the vacationing habits of a nation. In the past travelers wanted luxury, today they simply want a clean room and a comfortable bed—plus a color TV, of course.

Most of the chains that operate across the country can be depended on for consistency. When you book a reservation in a Howard Johnson's, Holiday Inn, or Ramada Inn, you have a fairly accurate idea of your accommodations. This is one of the major advantages of a chain motel. Another advantage is free guidebooks. Once you stay in a motel and determine that it suits your tastes and wallet you have only to ask for a free directory of the chain's motels across the nation. Another advantage is the toll-free reservation number. Before making any long-distance calls check to determine if a toll-free number is given. Even if not, you can still save the price of the call by letting a local member of the chain phone in the reservation for you.

Another means of saving money and at the same time determining something about the motel's standards is by looking for the display of certain symbols. Groups such as the AAA Motor Club, Best Western, Superior Motels, and the Master Hosts establish certain guidelines to be followed by their member motels. While these guidelines can assure you of cleanliness, the factors of price or beauty may vary. Some member motels are quite expensive. Others are in the budget category. The member insignia tells you only that the motel meets the *minimum* standards set up by the organization. Staying at one of these motels assures you of some clout if anything does go wrong. Not only can you complain to the manager, you can also ask the endorsing group to investigate. These groups publish directories and by using them you can learn a great deal about a motel before making reservations.

In recent years we have seen another innovation in motels. By cutting down on some services, chains such as Econo-Travel, Days Inn, and Suisse Chalet can offer prices more suitable to family budgets. If you simply want a clean room and a good bed, these motels may suit you exactly. However, if you want to stay next door to a major tourist attraction, or if you must have a swimming pool or color television, check before you make your reservation. Most of the budget motels have these niceties but some do not. Since these motels are quite reasonable, they fill up early. If you are planning to stay in one, make guaranteed reservations well in advance.

Another choice in lodgings is provided by the independent motel. Often these motels are family operations, and since there is no chain reputation to guide you, a listing in a directory may be doubly important. To be on the safe side, ask to see the room *before* you register.

3. Hotels. Most hotels are not a good choice for the budget conscious vacationing family. Hotels are usually located near airports or mid-city, frequently miles from where you want to sightsee. Also, while hotels offer such luxuries as meals served in your room, maids who will press your suit, and even bellhops to carry your luggage, you will be paying dearly for the pampering.

4. Cottages. One of the best ways to cut vacation costs is by renting a cottage and staying put for a week or more. Since many so-called cottages are quite spacious, two small families could save by sharing a cottage and splitting the cost of accommodations.

The advantage of the cottage is twofold. First, you save because you don't spend time driving from here to there. Secondly, you save money by doing your own cooking.

The most economical cottages are those which are owned and operated by either the National Park Service or the state. Check with the state park commission in the state you wish to visit, and, in most cases, you will be sent a free list of all parks with cottages available. The only problem is that these cottages are quite popular and it may be necessary to book for the summer months anywhere from six months to a year in advance.

5. Tourist homes. It is still possible to stay in a private home and be treated as a guest rather than as a paying customer. Being a "guest," however, is usually more expensive than being a customer in a nearby motel.

In the past, tourist homes tended to be for the vacationer who was looking for a bargain instead of atmosphere. Now, however, a new trend has developed in the tourist home business and the operation has become quite sophisticated. Businesslike couples have replaced the kindly old grandmothers on Social Security who previously ran tourist homes.

If you do like the rather novel idea of staying in a tourist home, be prepared to pay somewhat more than you would in a comparable motel or hotel. Also, check carefully before making reservations. Ask the proprietor of the tourist home if he is a member of the Tourist Homes Association. This organization sets standards for its members just as organizations such as Best Western set standards for motels.

Everybody Has to Eat

While entertainment, gasoline, lodging, and clothing take big bites from the family vacation budget, nothing puts quite the dent in it that meals do. Here are some tips for cutting vacation food costs:

1. Eat before you go. Certainly everybody is excited about leaving on vacation, but if you set them down for a good, balanced breakfast you actually save time and money. You can make the meal faster than the restaurant can, and bacon and eggs at "Mama's Place" costs about one-fourth as much as it would in a restaurant.

2. Pack a picnic lunch. With all the roadside parks conveniently located along interstate highways it makes good sense to carry your own lunch.

3. Plan on making your own breakfasts. Those little two-cup capacity pots which heat water in only a few minutes are a necessity for the traveler who wants to save money. In these pots you can heat water for tea, coffee, cocoa, bouillon cube soup, instant grits, instant oatmeal, or even instant macaroni products.

If you have enough space in your car, add such items as powdered milk, a portable grill, a box of cereal, or even a two patty electric hamburger maker. The flat side can be used for cooking bacon and eggs and the round side for hamburger patties.

Since most motels won't allow guests to fill their ice chests, I've found a way to utilize the ice they will let me have. We have a gallon thermos bottle which will hold mustard, ketchup, and mayonnaise in small plastic cups, plus a bottle of liquid margarine. After these items are put in the thermos I put in ice and then carefully add a plastic bag containing a few slices of bacon, and finish up with three eggs to be used for the first morning's breakfast.

4. Cook out. With the cheap, throw-away, fold-up type grill, which takes hardly any room at all in the trunk of a car, you can save substantially on vacation meals. Since these small grills are designed for take-along purposes, they usually last only one season. But they are so low priced it is still possible to economize on meals.

5. Have picnics. If you carry your own mustard, ketchup, and mayonnaise, the purchase of a loaf of bread and a package of sandwich meat can save you the price of lunch. Before you buy, however, take a vote to determine whether to have bologna or deviled ham and then plan so there are no leftovers.

6. Eat in familiar restaurants. All cooks occasionally have an off day, but must they do it when you are hungry and tired from sightseeing? Nothing is more disappointing than to sit down to a meal and discover that it is all wrong. To minimize this feeling, try sticking with the restaurants you know have standardized cooking measures. While Kentucky Fried Chicken and McDonald's don't serve gourmet fare, they are predictable and cheap.

7. Eat one good meal each day. One money-saving method of eating on vacation consists of eating a breakfast made in your room, eating a cheap lunch at Burger King or a similar place, and then making up for nutritional deficiencies by eating a good, balanced meal for dinner.

Another way of saving money is by temporarily becoming a vegetarian, at least during lunchtime. Many restaurants offer an "all you can eat" salad bar at lunchtime which includes such things as bean salad, eggs, cheese, and other salad fixings. Many times these restaurants have lunchtime specials, and, for the price of a hamburger and french fries, you can have a nutritious meal.

8. Plan your luxuries. If you are ever in an area with a restaurant so famous and so luxurious that you feel you *must* take it in, but you know you can't afford the prices, try an alternative. Lunches are generally lower in price than dinners are, so schedule your luxury for mid-day rather than evening. If even that is more than your budget can take, go for mid-afternoon pie and coffee instead. Certainly, you will spend more for that snack than a meal will cost elsewhere, but that tiny bit of luxury may make penny-pinching less of a chore during the rest of the trip.

Staying at Home for Vacation

Incredible as it may seem, one of the best places to take a vacation is in your own home. The surroundings conform to your notions of cleanliness and order, the beds fit your body just right, and the price can't be beat. Yet most people who can't go away for their two weeks of rest and relaxation feel truly deprived. If you can't afford to go someplace exotic, two weeks at home need not make you feel underprivileged if you remember that vacation is an attitude, not a place.

Here are some ways of turning that vacation at home into a real pleasure:

1. Remember you are on vacation. While you will no doubt want to make beds and do dishes, don't get carried away. You are on vacation so don't wash windows or clean out the attic. You wouldn't do those things if you had a round-trip ticket to London, would you?

2. See that others remember you are on vacation. One of the worst things about a vacation at home is the problem you will encounter in convincing other people that you are on vacation. Say no to the lady who wants you to collect for the endangered species fund. Don't answer the phone if you don't want to. (If you were a thousand miles away in a motel, you would never know your friend Martha wanted your recipe for hamburger casserole and that wouldn't give you a guilty conscience at all, would it?)

3. *Explore.* Unless your current address is Antarctica, you are probably no more than a hundred miles from an interesting sight. Since a two-hundred-mile round trip can easily be made in a day, plan to see what is in your area. To make it even more fun buy a tourist guide-book for your region listing all the nearby attractions and explore with the fresh viewpoint of a tourist.

4. *Learn the pleasures of simple things.* Who said a vacation has to be expensive to be fun? Try some of the free entertainment in your vicinity. Take the children on a picnic. Get some cane poles and go fishing. Participate in some of the library's activities. These might range from decoupage classes to travel movies to story hour for preschoolers.

5. *Do some of the socializing you have been putting off.* Have you been wanting to invite your cousin over for dinner, but there was never enough time? Do it during your vacation. Plan a simple cookout that won't put any pressure on you and catch up on all those invitations you have been meaning to return.

9

Turning a House into a Home

You And Your Home

A home is much more than just a place to live. The word *home* embodies a feeling of love, warmth, and family togetherness. Because of the warm images conveyed by the word, real estate salespeople have learned the benefit of using the word *home* to replace the more sterile sounding *house*. But in reality, only a house can be bought; a home must be created by the family who lives within that house.

A great deal of money is spent in buying, maintaining, and decorating the home. More money is spent on the home than on any other single endeavor. The amount of money spent on cars and groceries doesn't even compare with the cost of putting a roof over the family's head.

Whether you live in a house, apartment, condominium, or duplex, the amount of money to be spent is considerable. Though the renter is spared the expense of maintenance and taxes, renting is still expensive. Renters spend money on utilities, draperies, and furniture whether located in a one-family house or a multi-family apartment complex.

To a large extent, the money you spend on your place of habitation is a reflection of your values. Some families put such a high priority on living in a large, prestigious looking home that they are willing to sacrifice just about anything to accomplish this goal. Others don't pay much attention to their surroundings. As long as the plumbing works and roof doesn't leak, they give little thought to the surrounding walls. Still others, putting matters into perspective, care about their dwelling place, but, realizing that the home is the family instead of the house, do not obtain a house or an expensive apartment at the cost of sacrificing family values.

In Chapter One we saw that money is the cause of divorce in 70 percent of all broken marriages. Within this 70 percent lies another statistic: a large portion of these couples got into deep water financially because of their attitude about their place of abode. While it is true that expensive cars or a desire for fine clothes can be the cause of many financial problems, more often the culprit is the house. Owning one's own house is considered the ultimate sign of success in some areas. Even if that house is not well built and has a price tag far exceeding its value, someone will want it as a sign of his success.

In far too many instances young married couples get into financial trouble by wanting this sign of success immediately. While former generations toiled for years to scrape together a down payment, today's young marrieds want no part of such an arrangement. Instead, they will put down a small amount, secure a loan, and then take a second mortgage to cover the amount still lacking. Once they are in the house, they will eagerly use their charge accounts to furnish the house in a manner consistent with what their parents have after twenty-five years of marriage.

Usually the wife is the cause of this emotional leap into home ownership. A woman has special feelings about her home, a special quality which God intended women to have, but these feelings must be governed and not allowed to override good sense.

Owning a house has many benefits, but it is not always the

perfect solution. Even an ability to meet the house payments does not guarantee freedom from financial problems. For the homeowner there is always the matter of maintenance and unexpected repair bills. A great many couples find themselves financially pressured because of such things as a flooded basement or a leaky roof. Then they longingly think of days spent in an apartment where the headache was someone else's problem.

Many couples fail to take into account the possibility that the wife may not be able to work indefinitely. Often an unplanned pregnancy can be the start of a downhill slide. Not only does the child add a new expense but income is cut.

Before taking the leap into owning a house of your own, consider these guidelines:

1. Why do I want this house? The reason you verbalize and the reason you keep tucked deep inside may be vastly different. You may say you want to build some security, want to stop throwing money away on rent, or want to put down roots, but perhaps the real reason you want a house is to impress others or to bolster your feelings of inferiority. Before you sign on the dotted line, think this matter through completely and know exactly why you must have a house. By understanding your own feelings you will have a more accurate means of deciding whether or not the purchase is a good idea.

2. Can I afford it? Like any other bargain, a house is not a bargain if you cannot afford it. You may come across an owner who is desperate to sell his mansion at half price, but if that is more than you can afford forget it.

3. Can I afford the extras? A house is only the beginning of your homeowning expenses. You will need such things as a lawnmower, ladder, wheelbarrow, garden hose, trash cans, wrenches, hammers, pruning shears, draperies, a mailbox, and perhaps a fence. If you have previously lived in an apartment and are planning to move into a house without kitchen built-ins, add the cost of appliances as well. If the house is newly built, you will need grass seed, fertilizer, and maybe even some shrubs and trees.

Moving into a house necessitates having utilities listed in your name. You may have to pay for such things as phone installment, gas hook-up, and electric, water, sewer, and garbage service.

4. Can I afford the maintenance? Houses always need painting. By the time you finish the inside, it is time to start on the outside. Then the patio will need painting and the rust spots on the wrought iron railing must be dealt with immediately.

Of course, painting is not the most expensive undertaking. The mind-boggling expenses are those which occur unexpectedly: a furnace that stops working on a five-degree morning when mother and baby are due to come home from the hospital; a hot water heater that gives up in the middle of winter; a broken water pipe that floods the kitchen and makes replacing the kitchen floor a necessity; a root growth in the plumbing that causes sewage to back up into your bathtub. These are just a few of the "normal" things which have happened to us during our fifteen years of home ownership. After seeing some of the things which have happened to other home owners, I would say our experiences are more or less typical.

Some maintenance projects aren't this urgent, but, nevertheless, are expensive. Perhaps a tree which has been killed by insects must be removed or inadequate wiring or rusty pipes have to be replaced. These projects can drain the household budget.

5. Can I afford the lifestyle? Neighborhoods, like people, have differing personalities. Know before you move what kind of neighborhood you are getting into. Even if you can afford the house itself, can you afford the professional lawn care service that will be expected of you? In some neighborhoods things such as this take on a great importance to the other residents. If you can't drive a car equal to theirs or can't pay for the services of landscapers and interior designers, you might find it hard to be accepted into the neighborhood. A less demanding spot may be more to your liking.

6. Is the location acceptable? Among real estate salespeople there is a phrase which is often repeated: The three most important things about buying a house are location, location, and location. You can paint the exterior, add a room, knock out a wall, build in cabinets, or change the house in any number of imaginative ways, but the one factor which remains constant is the location. Consider it well before signing any contracts.

Know what zoning laws are in effect in your neighborhood. In particular, find out what is to be done with nearby parcels of unused land—you could find yourself sitting next to a factory, ball park, or liquor store.

Check traffic patterns, too. Dead-end streets and streets that don't form straight connections with main thoroughfares are the quietest. Find out about airplane traffic, and know how close railroad tracks are. Before signing any papers, drive around the neighborhood and know precisely what is within at least a one-mile radius of your intended house. Try visiting the house at different times of day. Perhaps the airplanes only fly over in the afternoon or the nearby fire station tries out its siren at only six in the morning. If you visit only in midday or at night you will not be aware of these things until too late.

7. Can I accept waiting for the things I want? Usually one of the main reasons for buying a house is in order to have more room. The only problem is, once you have more room you may not have enough furniture to fill that space. Can you wait patiently to be able to afford the extra furniture, or does the thought of empty unused space embarrass you? If so, it might be wise to postpone house buying until you have the funds to take care of that extra space.

8. Can I afford the utility bills? Find out exactly what kind of utility bills you will be paying *before* you buy a house. While a number of years ago it was the fashion to build "total electric" houses, the decision to buy a house such as this could cost you a great deal of money now. Know whether the city collects garbage or whether you must contract with a private firm. Know whether the water you will use comes from the city or county and how that effects rates.

9. Is the house sound? Don't wait until you move in to discover termites or a flooded basement or a leaky roof. If a seller won't let you examine the house before you commit yourself to buying it is likely he has something to hide. If you aren't knowledgeable about such matters, hire a professional house inspector. For about two hundred dollars these inspectors will thoroughly investigate a house and will tell you precisely what its strong and weak points are. Two hundred dollars spent on a house you didn't buy may seem a waste of money, but in the long run it is a bargain. Isn't it better to "waste" two hundred dollars and discover that the basement floor and the plumbing will have to be replaced than to buy without knowing and find yourself facing a bill of up to $10,000 for repairs?

Along with a sound house, you will want a sound title. Have a title insurance company run a check for any possible encumbrances. You don't want any long lost heir of the previous owner suddenly arriving on your doorstep and announcing that he is evicting you from *his* house.

10. Have I gotten the best possible deal? Buying a house is probably the most risky financial deal you will ever undertake. Remember, buyers may ask any price they wish for a house. While lenders will not finance an amount that is totally out of line, you can still make a mistake of several thousand dollars if not careful. The best defense is to hire your own appraiser and then make an offer considerably below what the owner is asking. After you raise your price and he lowers his price, you can probably come to a mutually acceptable mid-point.

Shop around for your home loan. Weigh the advantages of a VA loan, FHA loan, or conventional loan. Decide whether the lower payments required for a thirty-year loan will offset the advantage offered by a twenty-year mortgage. Don't fail to investigate each of your financing options.

Maintenance

It costs almost as much to maintain a home as it does to pay the mortgage payment. Some of the maintenance is purely cosmetic, but other aspects are vital and these are the ones which can cut the most deeply into your budget.

Some kinds of maintenance fall into the "as soon as we can afford it" category, but always take care of maintenance chores as soon as possible before they grow into larger problems. Paint the house before it needs scraping and requires twice as much paint. Replace missing shingles on the roof before the leak causes interior damage. Clear away the tree struck by lightning before it topples onto your garage roof. The most economical kind of maintenance is simply a matter of using common sense.

Another aspect of maintenance is upgrading what you already have. This might mean adding storm windows, a larger hot water tank, or a new wiring system. Working these things into your budget on a yearly basis can help to avoid sudden expenses when you can least afford them.

A properly sealed and insulated house is a great energy saver but the process involved can be quite expensive. Work with such projects as this by budgeting expenses. Divide the needed work into sections. Choosing one inexpensive maintenance chore and one costlier one to do each year, as you can afford it, makes it possible to eventually complete the job. For instance, if your house needs some energy-saving measures you might start by insulating the hot water tank, a relatively inexpensive measure, and the same year add storm doors, which costs considerably more. Another year insulation could be added to the attic and water pipes could be wrapped.

Most maintenance chores can be handled by do-it-yourselfers. Go to the library to find specific information on how to do a job. Go to the building supply company and ask questions about the products you will be buying. Utilize the informative brochures given away by many manufacturers. Above all, ask advice from friends who have performed the same maintenance chore you have in mind.

Of course, there will be certain jobs you will balk at doing, but even those chores can be done less expensively by bartering rather than paying cash. If climbing onto the roof is not your idea of a fun way to spend Saturday afternoon, ask your friends. Perhaps someone you know doesn't mind patching a roof but detests mowing the lawn. A talent swap can keep both of you happy. Use your skills imaginatively. There is no way to know if a barter can be used unless you ask. For instance, a whole section of our living room ceiling had to be replaced so we called in a friend who has a dry wall business. When asked his price, he told us he would rather have goods than cash. He asked if I would consider sewing him two shirts in exchange for the labor on the ceiling. Since the ceiling repair was worth about fifty dollars, his suggestion was good for both of us.

If, in spite of your desire to save cash you do not have either the health or the bravery necessary to do your own maintenance chores, there is still a less expensive alternative: in every neighborhood there seems to be at least one college student willing to do odd jobs.

Another type of payment for services is "salvage rights." Some people will cut down trees for you free of charge in order to get the wood for their fireplaces. Others will tear down old buildings in return for being allowed to keep the building materials. Ask around to see if a deal such as this can be arranged before you make a commitment to spend cash on maintenance chores at your house.

Money Down the Drain?

In some areas of the country utility bills have just about caught up with mortgage payments. Here are a few of the ways you might want to consider for saving money on gas, electricity, water, and the telephone bill:

Water. Most of us take clean water for granted, but like all other expenses the cost of water has risen. It costs money to maintain purification plants and to pay employees, so the price goes up as the cost of living rises. The only way to save money on water is to use less of it. One of the best ways to do this is by eliminating wasteful habits.

Do you leave the faucet running while you turn away for a few minutes to do other tasks? Encourage family members to turn the faucet off when water is not being used. Dripping water wastes hundreds of gallons of water a year, so take care of leaky faucets immediately. Take showers instead of baths because less water is needed that way. Don't wash half a load of dirty clothes. Wait until you have a full load for your washing machine. Each time the washer is used about thirty-five gallons of water go down the drain. A dishwasher, too, should be used only when it is full. While it uses only about five gallons of water—about the same amount used for hand-washing dishes a full load still makes the most economical use of your appliance.

One of the biggest users of your water supply is the bathroom toilet. Each time the tank is flushed as much as seven gallons of water are used. One means of cutting down on the amount of water used is by placing a brick in the tank to displace a portion of the water. Or you can buy a device which does the same thing. By cutting down on the amount of water in the tank the cost of each flush is lowered.

If you water your prize rose bushes or strawberries during dry summer months, you have probably noticed what this practice does to your water bill. In order to eliminate virtually all watering except during the driest times of the year, mulch heavily. Natural materials such as composted grass clippings, leaves, or pine straw help to hold moisture around the plant and keep it from requiring excess water.

Get in the habit of watering your house plants with "second-hand" water. The water in which you boiled some eggs is fine—after it has cooled down, of course. Even diluted tea is all right for some plants. If you wish, you can put tea leaves or coffee grounds around house plants to hold in their moisture and thus reduce their water requirement.

One of the biggest wasters of water are leaks. If your water bill seems to keep climbing, check your meter. If the measuring hand continues to move even when all water-using sources are inactive, you will likely need to call the water department for repairs.

Washing the car is another way in which water is wasted. To cut down on excessive use, turn the hose off while the car is being soaped, and use a spray nozzle.

Telephone. Having telephones in various rooms is a great convenience, but do you need as many extensions as you currently have? Since each one is adding to your monthly bill, try eliminating extensions you don't need. If your traffic patterns seem to fluctuate, ask the telephone company about the price of installing outlets for telephone jacks. Then you can use fewer extensions but still enjoy the convenience of having the telephone where you need it.

By using timetables supplied by your telephone system you can determine the most advantageous times to place long-distance calls. Usually the hours between eleven at night and eight in the morning have the lowest prices. Remember to take advantage of time differences, too.

Electricity. Cutting the cost of electricity can be dealt with in only two ways: eliminate it or use it efficiently.

Under the category of eliminations are such things as shutting off lights when you leave a room and turning off the television set when no one is watching. If you have one of the "instant on" sets, unplug it, too, because even when it is turned off it is using energy. While these measures might seem insignificant, they do offer a starting point for your program of energy reduction.

If you have a choice of electric heat or natural gas heat, natural gas is currently less expensive. However, since the future of energy supplies is a bit uncertain, it remains to be seen whether this price gap will continue to exist. If electricity must be generated by the power plant's burning of fuel oil, then the cost of electricity will continue to rise. However, if cheaper means of generating electricity—such as through the use of hydroelectric power—becomes widespread, then the price could stabilize. Right now, natural gas is cheaper to use because of the domestic supply we have in this country. As our own supplies are used up, however, we may find ourselves turning more toward foreign sources, resulting in rising costs.

If you cook with electricity, learn to utilize the fact that burners remain warm for a while after the controls are turned off. Time your cooking so that the residual heat finishes the job for you. When baking, preheat the oven only for foods which require it. Preheat no longer than the manufacturer recommends, usually about ten minutes. By experimentation you can discover for yourself just how long it takes to reach the temperatures you use most often. After baking turn the oven off immediately.

If you plan to buy new electrical appliances, one of the best ways to save money on future electric bills is by learning to carefully compare the energy guide labels which manufacturers are now required by law to put on new appliances. This label will give you an approximate estimation of what the appliance will cost you to operate for a year. Since kilowatt rates vary in different parts of the country, the label will show how much the yearly cost will be, based on kilowatt rates from two cents to twelve cents per kilowatt hour. Knowing your local rate will help you to decide if the appliance offers an energy bargain for you or not. If the appliance is one which uses both electricity and gas—such as a gas clothes dryer—the label will show operating costs for both. Since it is difficult to estimate furnace and air conditioner usage because of climate differences, estimation is done by the use of efficiency ratings. On an air conditioner, for example, the rating for the least efficient model is given, as is the rate for the most efficient model. The model being sold is assigned an efficiency number somewhere between these two extremes. The higher the number, the more economical the appliance will be to operate.

Gas. If your home is heated by gas, one of the best means of cutting costs is to buy appliances without automatic pilot lights. Investing in pilotless appliances can save you a great deal in operating costs during coming years. The pilot light on a gas dryer costs as much to operate—since it is going even when the dryer is not operating—as you will be paying for the actual clothes drying you do.

Gas stoves, too, have pilot lights which add to fuel consumption by operating constantly. A typical range with three pilot lights will use twice as much energy as an electric range, but since gas rates are lower than electric rates prices may be similar. A stove with pilot lights gives off heat at all times. While this is an advantage in the winter, it will increase the cost of summertime cooling.

Self-cleaning ovens, whether gas or electric, use a great deal of energy, particularly if you have the type which must reach temperatures of up to nine hundred degrees in order to do the job. If you have this type of oven, try to time the cleaning at the time of day when the heat generated will be the least detrimental. It should not be used during the hottest part of the day when the air conditioner is already struggling to maintain a cool temperature.

Having a serviceman check your gas appliances to regulate the flame on them is a good way to lower utility costs. If the flame on any appliance is not burning with a steady blue color, it is an indication that the gas is not being burned efficiently.

Furniture and Appliances

It takes a great deal of time, effort, and money to furnish a house. Even a small house requires a large investment in order to fill it with the comforts and conveniences most of us require. How, then, can this expense be pared by bargain hunting? Let's look at some of the ways of cutting furnishing costs:

1. Be sure of your choice. In every home there is probably at least one appliance or piece of furniture which nobody likes, but which continues to be used year after year. After all, it was a bargain, wasn't it? When buying furniture and appliances it is better to be sure you are getting what you want even if you do have to pay slightly more. Price should not be the only factor influencing you to buy something which costs several hundred dollars and will be in your home for as much as fifteen or twenty years. Know what you want and then bargain hunt to get your choice at the best possible price. It is not good bargain hunting to buy something you will dislike and discard before it is worn out.

2. Learn shopping alternatives. If you think a furniture store is the only place that sells furniture you are missing many money saving opportunities. Look in department stores, outlet stores, warehouse sales, flea markets, surplus stores, second-hand stores, office supply stores, and import stores.

If rattan objects are on your shopping list head for the import stores. Prices there are about one-third of those charged by furniture stores for similar pieces.

Another gold mine for the bargain hunter is found in the classified ads of the newspaper. People are always moving or getting rid of furniture for one reason or another. Regardless of what you want to buy, it will probably turn up in the classified section sooner or later.

Another seemingly unlikely place to shop is at the Post Office, but bargains can be found in this manner. Twice a year the Post Office Department auctions off items it has collected as the result of insurance claims. Almost anything is likely to turn up here, particularly things which can be mailed as gifts, such as blenders, toasters, and other small appliances.

Some major department stores have warehouses where damaged or one-of-a-kind goods are sold for amazingly low prices. In such places it is possible to buy mismatched bedding at about half what a comparable set of perfectly matched pieces would cost you. If you need a chair or a small table for your plants, these can frequently be had at bargain prices, too. Seasonal furniture in particular is a good buy at this kind of store. The price of patio furniture is often cut in half after the first frost of autumn.

Unfinished furniture usually is not a bargain. It is generally constructed of inferior materials and is not put together as solidly as finished furniture. For a similar price you can, with good shopping habits, buy quality finished furniture instead.

3. Know quality. Only by knowing good furniture or appliances when you see them can you assure yourself of worthwhile bargains. Brand names are not a reliable measure of a piece of furniture's craftmanship because most manufacturers make at least three price ranges of furniture.

A great many flaws can be hidden beneath upholstery. By reading a reliable book on furniture construction and by learning how to determine whether the pieces you want are well made, you can train yourself to recognize quality even if it is hidden beneath the upholstery. You will encounter such terms as decking, hardwood, hardboard, veneer, and dovetailing, and you will need to know the meaning of each in order to buy wisely.

Once you know what to look for in furniture, you are much more likely to know a bargain when you see one. Even if a piece of furniture contains a private label rather than a name brand, you can determine if it has been well made if you have done your homework. Major stores which have their own private lines of furniture and appliances do not manufacture their own. Instead, they contract with a well-known manufacturer who makes the product to the store's specifications and applies the private label.

4. Know price. Your best weapon against being overcharged is a thorough knowledge of current prices. If you watch the newspaper advertisements you will have a good idea of what the furniture or appliance you are seeking regularly sells for. Don't trust a sale price that is advertised simply as "40 percent off." Know the price and then you can judge for yourself whether the sale is worthwhile.

5. Take advantage of model changes. While it may be prestigious to buy a new car as soon as the model changes in the fall, there is absolutely no prestige in buying the latest model refrigerator simply because the new ones are available. As long as the refrigerator meets your criteria regarding price, value, color, and size, do you really care if it is last year's model? Model changes in appliances and furniture mean little to the consumer in terms of either performance or prestige, but it does mean a price cut on appliances already in stock.

Even sofas and chairs go through model changes. One year plaid sofas are "in" and the next year cut velvet is what everyone adores. One year Mediterranean furniture is the rage and the next year Victorian is all that is selling. By knowing what you like you can avoid the confusion and take advantage of the style changes. Select a basic style that will please you in coming years and don't bother with whether what you like is "in" or not.

10

"Tis the Season . . ."

The Financial Burden of Christmas

Is December 25 the actual birthday of Jesus? Biblical scholars see no reason to believe that it is. But most Christians see no harm in setting aside this day as a remembrance of our Savior's birth.

Giving is a joyful part of Christmas, but many have an improper perspective on gift giving. Why do you give Christmas presents? Do you see giving as an expression of love both for your Savior and for the person to whom the gift is given, or do you see it as a dreaded ritual that must be endured each year?

During a recent Christmas season while standing in a line to pay for my purchases, I noticed that practically everyone was laden with gift items. Most of the people waiting were shifting about impatiently and muttering such things as, "It doesn't matter what I give her anyway because she's going to exchange it" and "Uncle Joe really gets on my nerves but I figure I'd better give him a Christmas present." Where is the joy in this kind of giving?

Examine your ideas about Christmas giving and then you will be able to more adequately decide how to trim costs without destroying the beauty of Christmas' meaning.

A good way to begin is by refusing to fall victim to the buying syndrome. Being constantly bombarded with advertising makes it difficult to resist being caught up in the buying spree. Children, especially, are vulnerable to advertising, particularly on television. Of course, this is well known by toy manufacturers. How do parents counteract this problem? First, limit television viewing. Second, don't allow yourself to be drawn into the "everybody else has one" argument. Third, allow your child one television-promoted toy, and fill in with balls, jump ropes, puzzles, etc. He will become a more value conscious consumer when he is forced to make a choice. Afterwards he probably will notice that the ball, jump rope, and puzzles are more entertaining than the over-priced toy he thought was so necessary to his well-being.

Our children deserve the best. Let's give it to them in the form of more love and a deeper sense of real values with the opportunity for them to learn to be wise consumers and good stewards simultaneously.

Dealing with the Dilemma

Those of you with numerous brothers, sisters, nieces and nephews know that Christmas gift giving can be expensive. Here are some ways to cut expenses:

*1. **Draw names.*** In some families the entire clan gathers, usually on Thanksgiving Day, and everybody's name is put into a hat. Those who are not able to be present choose a proxy to draw for them. Everyone takes a name from the hat and buys a gift for that person. In most families, however, the grandparents are excluded from the drawing as most of the children and grandchildren want to continue giving separate gifts to them.

In some large families, two or three drawings are held. The adults swap names among themselves and the teenagers have their own drawing, as do those under twelve. Usually a price limit is set in order to equalize the spending.

2. *Give presents only to the children.* In some other families the adults do not give each other gifts. Instead each aunt and uncle gives gifts to all the nieces and nephews. This idea does have some shortcomings. If not handled with the greatest of care, this method may develop into a "have to" situation. An added problem is that the children take the gift giving for granted.

3. *Eliminate Christmas giving among the extended family.* While doing away with Christmas gift exchanging might seem radical, some families are finding it to be the best solution. By shifting from Christmas giving to birthday giving many are finding more pleasure in the giving. A child with many aunts and uncles may pay little attention to extra gifts received at Christmastime, but the special attention he receives on his birthday means a great deal more.

4. *Give things other than gifts.* Would your sister enjoy having a baby sitter for an afternoon so that she might complete her Christmas shopping? Would your brother enjoy having his car washed and waxed? How about giving your mother freedom from Christmas cooking chores by organizing the family get-together into a covered dish affair?

5. *Consolidate funds.* In several large families all the brothers and sisters contribute toward some special present for the parents. The dollar amount may be whatever is comfortable for the various members of the group, but by consolidating their funds they are able to give a more expensive present than they could have given separately. Depending on the number of participants and the amount each can comfortably give, the gift might range from a food processor to

an all-expense paid vacation. The key to this kind of giving is to be sure it is what everyone wants to give and that the amount each must contribute is affordable. A financial pinch takes the joy out of the giving.

Pre-planning

Like any other aspect of the budget-conscious homemaker's life, gift giving can be more enjoyable with pre-planning. By spotting potential Christmas gifts in advance, it is possible to make gift dollars go much further. The same goes for birthday, wedding, and anniversary gifts.

The first step in pre-planning is deciding how many gifts you will need throughout the year. Write down every birthday and anniversary you will buy for and approximately what you intend to spend. Then, thinking back to previous years, try to reach a reasonable estimate of how many graduation invitations, wedding invitations, and baby shower invitations you are likely to receive. Also include any other special events for which you normally purchase gifts such as Mother's Day, Father's Day, and Teacher Appreciation Day. When all these gifts are listed and an appropriate amount decided on for each, total the amounts and divide by twelve. This is the minimum you will need to budget for gift giving expenses each month. When you first start to budget your gift expenses add a bit more. Until you become accustomed to buying ahead and in anticipation of unknown gift situations you are going to need a little extra to see you through. As soon as you set up your first budget, three birthdays will inevitably arrive before you have time to build a surplus.

January is the best gift buying month. Of course, linens will be on sale, but don't overlook the bargains in other departments as well. After Christmas many stores mark down perfume sets and leather goods. Clothing is on sale, too, but buying clothing in advance can be a bit risky unless you are very sure of the size and color preference of the person you intend to give the gift.

My best shopping place is my own "store." Throughout the year I buy gift items which are on sale and store them in a drawer set aside for that purpose. Then when I need an unexpected gift, I can reach into the drawer and pull out perfume, stationary, a wallet, or a pen set.

Any mother with young children will feel the financial strain caused by the innumerable birthday parties to which grade school children are invited. Try to keep a stock of games, puzzles, and coloring books just for this purpose. While these items may seem like small expenditures, they can dent your budget if several birthdays fall within the same month.

Another method of controlling your gift budget is by not buying according to price but according to item. Suppose you have planned to give your mother a birthday present that costs $25.00. Certainly, you want the best value for your money, but most importantly you want a gift that will please. Accordingly, you decide precisely what you will buy, but when you arrive at the store you discover that the item has been marked down to $12.50. The immediate temptation is to rejoice over the savings and then proceed to spend another $12.50 on a second present. However, since it is the thought that counts and that $12.50 item is exactly what she wants and just what you intended to buy, why not give her the gift and leave the unexpected bonus of the $12.50 you saved in your gift buying fund? There is no need to feel guilty. You wouldn't have felt obliged to buy her two presents if the first one had cost the $25.00 you originally planned to pay, would you?

Make It Yourself

One of the most satisfying means of cutting costs of gift giving is by making the gift yourself. If you intend to follow this plan the important questions to ask yourself are: Can I make this object well enough to avoid being embarrassed by giving it? Does the person to whom I plan to give this gift need it? Honestly answering these two questions before you begin can greatly increase your pleasure in giving the item. Realistically assess your talents and if you are not experienced enough to make the particular item you had in mind, practice before presenting the tangible result of your talent to someone else. Also, if the intended recipient likes Danish modern furniture and the uncluttered look, perhaps you had better cancel your plans to give her a hand-crocheted, triple-ruffled doily with a pineapple motif. Even if you are the world's most proficient crocheter the gift won't be appreciated if it isn't right for the recipient.

While most of us think of making gifts as a means of cutting costs, probably the real reason we make gifts is because of the enjoyment we get from the creative process. Making your own gifts may save you money but you deceive yourself if you think making all your gifts will cut your gift budget to nothing. The real savings in handmade gifts comes when you create something from "found" materials. A tabletop arrangement of flowers you have dried or a rag doll made from leftover fabric remnants are examples of this.

Children especially love making their own gifts, and, if you have the time and patience to see your preschooler through an afternoon devoted to scissors and glue, you will see a shining little face reflecting the new-found knowledge of just how delightful giving can be. I don't recommend giving your child's felt-covered soup cans which have been transformed into pencil cups to the entire neighborhood, but I can unequivocally recommend giving them to grandparents.

The Accessories

One of the biggest expenses involved in gift giving is the wrapping. In fact, if you make a gift yourself and manage to come out quite cheaply in that department you may realize with a shock that the gift wrap and card cost more than the gift. The solution?

Immediately after Christmas is the best time to buy Christmas wrap and cards but there is not an out-of-season time to buy birthday trimmings. However, with a little preplanning you can use Christmas wrap for other occasions. Silver foil is perfect for wedding presents. Red foil is just right for valentine gifts. Christmas ribbon and bow assortments can see you through an entire year of gift giving. White ribbon matches everything and gold ribbon is almost as versatile. Even red and green ribbon can be used if you can find birthday wrap with a predominance of these colors. Look in discount department stores for packages of assorted paper. For about the price of two sheets of name brand birthday paper, you can buy a package of twenty sheets of assorted gift wrap.

Don't overlook the fact that gift wrap doesn't necessarily have to be purchased at the stationary counter. Box your gift and use fabric as though it were gift wrap. Lightweight fabrics can be taped and heavier ones can be held in place by a basting stitch or two.

If you have budding artists in your family, let them do their coloring and painting on inexpensive butcher paper or even white sacks such as some department stores use. These "masterpieces" can then be used to gift wrap presents for grandparents or aunts and uncles. If you are giving a gift purchased with consolidated funds from a group, let everyone who has chipped in write a brief message on plain paper and then sign his name. This is particularly thoughtful for a going-away present.

Sacks can be effectively used to package bulky gift items. Simply insert the gift, staple the top of the sack and then decorate the improvised wrap. If you are handy with scissors and construction paper, you can create an appropriate scene or a "portrait" of the intended recipient. A silhouette cut from black construction paper makes a personalized gift and the silhouette can later be matted and framed.

If the grocery store is having a sale on shelf paper it may be cheaper than gift wrap. If you buy the solid colored kind you can embellish it with gold foil dots (try spelling out a name) sold in stationary stores or you can add a lacy effect with cheap paper doilies. Even boxes of inexpensive foil stars can be put to good use on gift wraps.

Did you know that wallpaper sample books are given away free by most stores that sell wallpaper? As soon as the patterns are discontinued the store has no further use for the books. Some of the pages which contain small flowers or juvenile prints are just right for gift wraps.

How to Give a Gift with Flair

On every Christmas morning hundreds of men must open boxes containing white shirts. They smile and say, "Hey, how about that! It's just what I needed." It might be just what they needed but it is doubtful the gift offered any thrill.

What is thrill value? It is the secret ingredient which makes the recipient know you took the time and made the effort to go beyond the expected in order to give him something special. These kinds of presents need not be expensive. This kind of giving boils down to understanding the person for whom the gift is intended. Your father might *need* a white shirt, but what he *wants* is new fishing lures.

Learn to recognize the signals and you, too, can learn to give gifts that will be long remembered even though they are not costly. For instance, does your sister complain that she can't find a cookbook of old-fashioned recipes? Perhaps in a year of scanning your old magazines you could collect a hundred or so of just the sort she would like. Organize them into a scrapbook and she will love her custom-made cookbook. Is your new sister-in-law homesick for the town she left when she married your brother? She would probably be thrilled about receiving a gift subscription to her hometown newspaper. Does your daughter enjoy ice skating shows? Some ice skating lessons might mean more to her than a new bike. Does your father regret that the only photograph of his grandfather is the one your uncle owns? Give his Father's Day a boost by getting a copy made of that old photograph.

Of course, real flair in gift giving comes from other factors, too. You can thrill a gift recipient by not only guessing what he truly wants but by showing flair in your choice of presents. Kits of all kinds are extremely popular, whether they be rug-making kits or stamp-collecting kits. The most satisfactory kit you will ever give is the one you assemble yourself. I learned this when I went into a fabric store to buy a sewing kit for a young friend leaving for college. For an outrageous price I could have obtained a ready-made kit containing a tape measure, scissors, pins, needles, thimble, a few spools of thread, and a needle threader. For half as much I bought her a good quality pair of scissors—the ones in the kit were ridiculously shoddy—plus all the other items as well. Another time I assembled a "kit" consisting of all sorts of baking pans for a bride-to-be. By choosing sale priced items I was able to give her a pizza pan, two loaf pans, two cake pans, a pie plate, and a sheet cake pan. My gift was the hit of the bridal shower. Of course, the young lady received many gifts which were more beautiful or costly, but my gift filled a need—her love of baking.

It is possible to put together almost any kind of kit for almost any occasion. For a baby shower you might fill a diaper bag with a jar of petroleum jelly, some diaper pins, baby powder, a baby care book, or a small box of disposable diapers. For a would-be stamp collector you can obtain a Post Office kit and add some used stamps of your own for extra interest. If you don't have access to foreign stamps look around for a place of business which might be willing to let you have empty envelopes. For a young gardener, provide a kit of garden tools and some hardy varieties of seeds, such as marigolds and zinnias.

Other ways to give a gift with more flair than expense is to give something totally unexpected. If your little niece is likely to get five dolls for her birthday from her other aunts and uncles, the gift she will like best is the unusual present you give her. Children love "grown-up" presents. For that reason if you give them things which they don't usually receive because of their age you have won a place in their childhood memories. I'm not advocating giving young girls eye shadow and hosiery, but you can give a pre-teen a cosmetics kit consisting of skin cream, perfumed soap, bath powder, and a colorless lip balm. For the child who enjoys scribbling try making up a kit of office supplies: envelopes, writing tablets, decals, a rubber address stamp, and—most important of all—some impressively grown-up looking legal paper, such as rent receipt pads or a ledger. A paper file box will complete the kit and will keep the recipient's mother happy, too.

There may be times when the greatest thrill of all comes in giving someone something which costs you nothing at all. Do you have a gold necklace you promised to give your daughter? Why wait until your will is read? If she is already a grown woman, a birthday gift of the family heirloom may bring her a great deal of joy which will be intensified since you are there to share it with her. "Used" gifts are perfectly acceptable if they are family heirlooms or gifts of sentimental value.

Do Instead of Buy

The most appreciated gift of all may be the intangible one you cannot gift wrap. Services are some of the most appreciated gifts of all. Such things as baby-sitting, shopping, or hair styling make welcome gifts. In particular service gifts are appreciated by older people who may already have all the bric-a-brac, clothing, and labor-saving devices they need. An offer to go to the Post Office for them occasionally may mean much more.

Sometimes a service can be combined with a purchased present. One year for my mother's birthday I bought a home permanent kit and spent an afternoon doing her hair. The cost of the permanent was small, but included in the gift was my time and the fact that the finished product represented a savings to her of at least thirty-five dollars, the price of a salon permanent.

Service gifts are especially nice for those people you would like to remember even though they are not a part of your gift list. Giving them the gift of your time brings happiness but does not obligate them to give a gift in return. Some ideas you may want to consider are taking a family of newcomers to your neighborhood on a drive to see all the Christmas lights or taking an older person out for a day of shopping and lunch.

A teacher friend once told me that the most appreciated gift she ever received came from a mother who must have understood how difficult it is to work all day, prepare dinner, and be back at school by seven o'clock for a PTA meeting. She was thrilled one afternoon to be presented with a ready-made casserole, some bread which only needed warming, and a luscious homemade dessert. While the teacher has forgotten most of the people who gave her perfume, handkerchiefs, and chocolates throughout the years, she hasn't forgotten that considerate woman who knew how to give an unusual gift.

Give of Yourself

One of the nicest gifts anyone can receive is the gift of your time. Even those of us on a budget can afford this kind of "shopping." It is not necessary to wait for a special holiday to do nice things for others. However, tying a gift of your time into a holiday season may help you put your own values into new perspective.

Two families in our church "adopted" a family of five children who had been removed from their mother's custody. While the children were being cared for in foster homes they were separated. By giving a Christmas dinner for these children and by providing them with toys and clothing these two families brought back some of the glow that they had lost during Christmases of previous years. With tears in her eyes, one of the women told me, "This year I finally realized what Christmas is all about."

Another way of remembering others at Christmas is through Christmas cards and letters. With the rising prices of both cards and postage this practice is becoming more and more costly. By buying cards during the after-Christmas clearance it is possible to save as much as fifty percent, but postage prices are still a problem. One alternative which can cut postage costs by one-third is to mail Christmas postcards instead of cards in envelopes. Sharing Christmas cards with only those who will truly appreciate them such as missionaries and the elderly, is another way of reminding yourself of the meaning of Christmas.

Even Fig Leaves Are Expensive Now

Clothing Doesn't Grow on Trees Anymore

Have you ever found yourself with barely enough money to cover necessary expenses, and one child comes home from school announcing that someone "borrowed" his new jacket while another child comes through the front door gleefully pointing out how three of his toes protrude through his worn old sneakers?

Even though such emergencies occur, a day like that is almost enough to make any mother gnash her teeth. Since it is hopelessly impossible to eliminate the problem of stolen jackets and worn sneakers, another alternative must be found. What can a mother do?

The answer lies in two directions: budgeting and preplanning. When families are having financial difficulties, one of the first things to suffer is the family clothing allowance. You reason, "I'll eliminate clothing expenditures temporarily until our finances improve and I'll go back to using the clothing allowance after we get straightened out again." The problem with this kind of thinking is that by the time you get "straightened out" again you will have become so accustomed to having that extra money in another fund that it is nearly impossible to get it back into a clothing fund.

Of course, if there are no children in your household and your wardrobe is in fairly good shape, you may be able to go a year without spending any money on clothing. However, with children in the household the clothing budget can be pared in many cases but cannot be eliminated. As a matter of fact, when children are growing rapidly it may be necessary to temporarily increase the clothing budget.

Once you accept the fact that you *must* budget for clothing expenditures, life becomes simpler. You may not need to buy anything at all during some months and the fund can be allowed to accumulate for back-to-school time. By having a budgeted amount for clothing, you can build yourself a "cushion" of funds for emergencies, such as a stolen jacket, or to stock up on needed items when you unexpectedly encounter a worthwhile sale. Nothing is more frustrating than finding an item you need marked down to half price and knowing your clothing allowance is gone.

Many people have problems with carrying easily accessible cash. They are tempted to buy anything that catches their eye. If that's your case, then forego unnecessary shopping excursions or leave your money at home. Clothing funds should be used for clothing and shoes only. Such things as earrings, scarves, and stickpins should be purchased with your personal funds.

Pre-planning

Are you taking inventory of each family member's wardrobe at least every three months? If not, you are missing an excellent opportunity to cut clothing costs. Pre-planning involves more than making a mental note that the children will be needing new summer things. Pre-planning means you will know several months in advance specifically what they will need. You will know the best colors to choose to stretch some still wearable separates from last year into usable outfits.

Certain seasons are better than others for buying particular items. If you are afraid to buy your rapidly growing son a coat in February when the prices are lowest, you can make a note to purchase the coat later in the year and use your February clothing allowance to stock up on underclothes and socks which are somewhat adaptable to size changes. Since back-to-school time is not the most advantageous time to find bargains, buy everything you can earlier in the year.

If outgrown clothing is to be passed to a younger child, make a note of that, too. By knowing specifically what you have to work with you can save money by coordinating your purchases with items already on hand. If the blouse your daughter wants comes in both blue and orange you will save money if you remember her sister has handed down a navy blue skirt to her. If you forget such things as that you will find yourself deducting the cost of a new orange blouse *and* a skirt to go with it.

On major items such as coats and shoes, it is good to be aware of potential problems before a "right now" emergency develops. If your son owns only one pair of sneakers, knowing about the thin spot in the fabric will help you to be alert for bargains before the day arrives when he comes home with three toes sticking out.

For the adults in the family, buying out of season is a vital means of cutting clothing costs. By knowing in advance that your winter coat won't last another season, or that your husband's dark blue suit is wearing out, you can be ready for the sales.

Knowing your family's gift buying habits can aid your clothing budget, too. Does your husband always give you a robe and a nightgown for Christmas? Does your mother always present you with lingerie for your birthday? How about the gifts the children receive? Pajamas, robes, sweaters, and shirts are popular Christmas presents in many families. If this is true in yours, try making do until the holidays if you anticipate such gifts. If they don't materialize as you expected you can take advantage of the January sales. If anyone asks what you would like, don't be shy. Most people want to give you a present you will truly like.

What Does My Family Need?

With the increasing interest in sports activities and casual wear, it is impossible to set up any specific clothing guidelines which would be acceptable for any so-called average family. You are the only one who can accurately gauge your family's needs. Do they like to dress up or would they rather wear casual clothes? Does your husband like to fish or does he prefer to be on the golf course? Does your teenage daughter like faded jeans or feminine dresses? All these factors will figure into your clothing decisions.

If you are in the habit of washing clothes only once a week you will need more socks and undergarments for your family than will the woman who washes daily. Also, if you speedily repair rips and missing buttons, less clothing will be needed because everything will be usable at the same time.

One of the best ways to use your clothing allowance wisely is to see your family as they are instead of as you mentally visualize them to be. No matter how good a bargain price seems the item is not a bargain if your family doesn't like it. For instance, my daughter would not wear the world's most expensive turtleneck sweater even if I managed to find it at the reduced price of ten cents. My husband would not wear a brown suit even if they were being sold at two for a dollar, complete with designer labels.

Making Clothing Last Longer

Many people think that nothing is as good as it was in those mythical "good old days" but today's clothing is actually much better. Yet, often a garment that seems well-made when we buy it doesn't come up to our expectations of length of service. Since a piece of clothing that wears out prematurely creates a dent in the clothing budget, one of the most profitable means a homemaker can find of stretching her clothing dollar is by ensuring that garments last as long as possible. Here are a few of the ways to accomplish this task:

1. Buy clothing suitable for the season and the activity. Make sure your family takes time to put on appropriate clothing for the activities they are engaging in. For example, be sure your son doesn't play football in his school clothing. Don't expect delicate fabrics to stand up to exertions they were never designed to take.

2. Don't wash clothes more than you need to wash them. Most of us wash a great many things that aren't dirty. The blouse your daughter wore for a half hour while she talked on the telephone could be hung back in her closet. The clean skirt you exchanged for your faded one for the trip to the store certainly isn't in need of washing. While keeping clothes clean helps to prolong their durability, each time a garment is washed the fiber is weakened. By all means wash what is dirty, but you will save more than detergent if you refrain from washing what is not dirty.

3. Make repairs immediately. We all know that Granny was right when she told us that "a stitch in time saves nine" but most of us would rather put off the job until all nine stitches are needed. A good time to check for needed repairs is when you are folding the laundry. Most rips are in predictable places, such as under the armhole seam, around the waistline, in the crotch seam of slacks, and around the hemline of dresses. It helps to enlist your family as repair spies, too.

4. Use care with fabric softener. One of the homemaker's best friend is her bottle of fabric softener but its overuse can be detrimental to clothing. The same thing is true of bleach. Use only the amount the manufacturer recommends. Overuse can weaken the fibers of the fabric.

5. Put your clothes properly away. Clothes left lying on the floor or across a bed aren't going to last as long no matter what your teenager chooses to believe. Hanging up dresses keeps the hemlines from sagging prematurely. Putting lingerie in drawers keeps hooks and snaps from damaging other garments with which they come in contact. Another hazard of littering clothing is that puppies and kittens can't tell the difference between the bed you made for them in the den and the bed they found for themselves on top of your clothing.

6. Buy clothes that fit. Few of us are a perfect size ten, but with careful shopping we can have clothing that fits well. Clothing that is too tight will bind and pull with the eventual result of rips or tears or even a shredding of the fibers near the seam line. Clothing that is too large will sag and fall into lines it was never meant to have. Once a garment loses its shape you won't want to wear it any longer even if it isn't worn out.

7. Don't wear out parts of an outfit. Separates are the greatest wardrobe stretchers, but to get maximum benefit from them they must be used wisely. For instance, at one time I had a suit which consisted of a navy blue jacket and skirt. With a little imagination and some switching of coordinates, that outfit could have seen a great deal of mileage. Unfortunately, I didn't plan ahead. The jacket was worn with the skirt maybe once a month, but I found myself reaching for the skirt nearly every week because it went so well with my red striped blouse, my blue flowered blouse, and my white blouse and red plaid vest. The result? The skirt wore out long before the jacket did. Of course, the jacket was still a useful part of my wardrobe, but I had lost the advantage of having a nicely matched suit. If a navy blue skirt was that essential to my wardrobe, I should have bought an extra one for pairing with all those other things. A single skirt would have cost far less than an entire suit.

What About Do-It-Yourself?

For the homemaker interested in cutting the clothing budget, sewing part of the family wardrobe is essential. Nevertheless, while sewing is a wonderful way to cut costs, making clothing is not something everyone likes to do. The woman who despises sewing should not feel guilty about her lack of fondness for the sewing machine. Instead, she can devote additional time and energy to finding ready-made bargains.

It is possible to cut clothing costs in half by making your own apparel, but most women who sew don't save anywhere near that much. The real joy of sewing comes from the feeling of creativity and in the pleasure of having a garment that fits. The woman who simply walks into a fabric store, selects a new pattern for each garment, buys her fabric in quantities specified on the pattern envelopes, and purchases all her sewing notions isn't saving much money. Many women who would not dream of buying other items in this manner think nothing of buying their sewing needs this way.

In order to save the maximum amount of money it is necessary to shop just as carefully for sewing needs as for ready-made items. Such tactics as waiting for the sales, buying at the end of the season, and buying from discount centers work just as well in the case of home sewing as they do for buying ready-made clothing.

Do you know how much sixty-inch wide fabric it takes to make yourself an A-line skirt or a long-sleeved blouse? Do you know how much forty-five inch fabric is needed for that house-dress pattern your mother likes so well? Only by knowing such things as this can you effectively shop "door-buster" sales. The store will be crowded with customers and whole bolts of fabric will disappear under your nose while you stand and ponder how much yardage you need. The solution I have found is to carry a small notebook which lists all my frequently used patterns. I have listed the yardage for an A-line skirt, wrap skirt, chevron stripe skirt, and various other basic items. Then when I see a sale priced item or remnant I know what can be done with it.

Patterns represent another big investment for the seamstress. With prices continuing to rise, particularly on designer patterns, it is necessary to use each pattern more than once for the maximum savings. Therefore, in choosing a pattern try to get one that contains more than one style. A choice of necklines or sleeves can make the pattern look totally different when sewn in various colors and fabrics. With a little practice a reasonably adept seamstress can learn to get by with fewer patterns. By sticking to basic designs and learning to take a collar or a sleeve from one pattern and incorporate it into the design of a different pattern you can become your own designer. The public library contains numerous books on sewing and most explain the art of using pattern parts interchangeably.

Notions are some of the biggest profit makers any fabric store handles. You may frequently see cloth on sale, but it is quite rare to find zippers, buttons, lace, and thread marked down. For this reason the home seamstress can save by ordering large quantities of these goods from discount mail order houses.

The biggest savings of all comes, not in sewing clothing, but in learning to make part of your gifts, home accessories, draperies, and even shower curtains. Anyone able to make a dress can probably do any of these other things as well.

How to Get the Most for Your Clothing Dollars

As most of us learn the hard way, price is not always an accurate gauge of quality. Sometimes the cheapest item is the best buy, but at other times the cheaper of two items is so shoddy that the higher priced one is the better bargain at even twice the price. No wonder shopping for clothing is such a chore!

How can the homemaker know if she is getting the most for her money when she buys her family's clothing? These are a few of the points worth checking as you shop:

1. Does the garment really fit? Baggy or tight clothes are not going to be comfortable to the wearer. No matter how low the price, a garment is not a bargain unless the fit is right. Necklines should not sag. Collars should lie flat. Sleeves should be the right length, and you should be able to flex your shoulders in comfort without ripping out the armhole seam. Too-long skirts can be easily hemmed up, but too-short skirts are a constant irritation to the wearer who must keep tugging at them. Waistlines are important, too. Nothing makes a garment more uncomfortable to wear than having the waistline too short. When buying slacks for the men in the family, select only those which have an adequately long crotch seam and a waist that will not gap when the wearer bends over.

2. Does the garment coordinate with the rest of your wardrobe? A sale priced garment is not a bargain if buying it means you will be compelled to buy other things to go with it. If it doesn't readily fit into your color scheme, it will become either an expensive addition to your wardrobe, or an unworn "white elephant."

3. Will this garment be hopelessly out-of-style in six months? Everybody enjoys wearing current styles, but excessively trendy items must be avoided by the budget conscious homemaker. A good, basic cut garment can be practically timeless, but a style setting garment dates quickly. Of course, nobody is going to stick strictly to classic styles, but even among current fashions some things stay around longer than others.

When I was in high school a popular television medical show brought about a new fashion: white blouses made to look just like doctors' lab coats. At first, I couldn't understand why my mother wouldn't let me have one of them, but in about two months I understood. By that time another fad was all the rage and nobody would be seen wearing an outdated imitation of a doctor's coat.

Common sense can be your guide in determining what fashions will last awhile and which are passing fads. For instance, if one or two men's shops are selling bell-bottomed slacks, then that is probably a trend that won't last long. If, however, you have to search to find a pair of slacks that are *not* bell-bottom, then it is probably a style that will be "in" for a reasonable length of time.

4. ***Can the garment be bought cheaper elsewhere?*** Sometimes in the thrill of having found *the* perfect coat or dress we can get carried away. But if the garment is so wonderful you feel you *must* have it, ask the clerk to hold it for you until the next day or pay the token amount necessary for putting the garment on lay-away. If you change your mind you will lose the lay-away fee, but losing this small amount is preferable to losing a more substantial amount because you didn't bargain hunt. Then, with the assurance that your heart's desire won't be purchased by another customer, you can visit other stores and see for yourself if something suitable is available at a better price.

5. ***What is the garment's purpose?*** Sooner or later almost every woman succumbs to the temptation to buy a beautiful garment which has no place in her wardrobe. While the price may be wonderful and the garment flawless it is no bargain if it doesn't fit your lifestyle. Before buying any specialty garment, such as an evening gown, golf skirt, or tennis dress, take your own lifestyle into consideration. If you haven't felt a pressing need for the garment in past months, it isn't likely you are going to need it much in future ones.

A Store Is Not the Only Place to Shop

When you need new clothing do you automatically jump into the car and drive to the nearest shopping center? If so, you are probably spending more on clothing purchases than you would if you shopped more carefully. A retail store is not the only place to buy clothes. By looking around you can find less expensive alternatives.

Outlet stores. Such firms as Sears and J.C. Penney have outlet or surplus stores to get rid of surplus and seasonal merchandise. Since the contents of these stores vary according to the season, you never know exactly what you will find. Therefore, it is not always easy to walk into one of these stores with the intention of buying a particular item. Generally these stores are places to consider when you want to buy out of season. Most of the merchandise is new, discontinued items from the catalogs. That means that summer apparel is available about the time the winter catalogs come out in late summer. The savings on discontinued catalog items are often exceptional. It is not unusual to see clothing marked down to less than 50 percent of its original price.

Army/Navy stores. While these sources are no longer quite the bargain hunter's dream they used to be before shoppers other than hunters and fishermen discovered them, it is still possible to find some worthwhile bargains. Navy pea jackets and khaki pants are perennial favorites. Many of these stores are becoming more diversified and are even offering some items which are not strictly military surplus. Many of the Army/Navy stores look a bit run down and the contents appear to have been arranged in a giant mixer, but the bargains are there if you are adventurous enough to look.

Garage sales. Surely by now, every person in the United States knows about garage sales. Clothing ranges in price from dirt cheap to rock bottom cheap and you will find more variety than in your local shopping center.

Goodwill and Salvation Army stores. If you aren't squeamish about buying used garments—and you shouldn't be if you've ever heard of soap and hot water—some fantastic bargains can be found in these stores. Although many used things are available, many spectacular bargains can be found on new clothing.

Around the first of the month companies donate surplus merchandise to these organizations, and if you are alert you can buy brand name new clothing for the price of a loaf of bread.

Another thing to look for in used clothing is recyclable parts. With the price of buttons steadily increasing, often the buttons alone are worth the asking price, even if you throw the garment away after removing the buttons. The same thing is true of appliques, laces, and other trims. You may find a practically new dress with an unrepairable hole in it. Is it a good buy? It is if it has enough material in the skirt to make another garment, such as a child's dress, a woman's blouse, or doll clothes.

Advertiser papers. Many neighborhoods now have classified ad newspapers. Often such items as party gowns, wedding gowns, baby clothes, and men's suits are offered at unbelievable low prices. To a certain extent shopping from these papers is like shopping at a garage sale—only you don't have to drive your car to do it. Many times advertisers offer garments worn only one or two times. You can find exceptional values even though the cost is generally going to be quite a bit higher than rummage sale prices.

Thrift shops. These operate on the same principle as the Goodwill and Salvation Army stores except that in many cases these stores are run by society ladies who use the funds to support their favorite charity. These clothes are secondhand but carry designer labels and most still have a hefty price tag. A $2000 designer dress marked down to "only" $150 is still not a bargain in my book, but among the overpriced specimens it is occasionally possible to find a wonderfully made garment at a reasonable price.

Manufacturers' outlets. If there are garment manufacturing firms in your area check with them to see if they have a retail store.

Usually manufacturers who also sell directly to the public will sell at about 25 percent discount. This is a good savings, but still it is necessary to exercise care. Certain items are occasionally marked down more during sales at discount department stores. The real bargains are seconds and irregulars—garments which are not quite up to company standards because of flaws. Care must be taken when buying seconds, but you can have great savings if you are willing to sew on a button, stitch up a ripped seam, or hide the fabric flaw with a bit of lace. Sometimes the problem is simply that the garment has a spot of sewing machine oil on it. Depending on the fabric, this may wash out.

Catalogs. It would be nearly impossible to find a home which does not contain at least one catalog since catalog shopping has become an accepted part of our shopping habits. However, if you haven't gone beyond the catalogs put out by Aldens, J.C. Penney, Sears, Spiegel, or Montgomery Wards, you haven't done much catalog exploring at all.

The savings in catalog shopping is not always the price. The advantage is convenience, particularly if you live a long way from a large city or want to purchase something difficult to find in stores. Did you know there are catalogs for women who wear size three shoes, catalogs for women who wear size twenty-four to fifty-two clothing, and even catalogs of Irish sweaters or hand-embroidered Mexican clothing? How can you find such specialized catalogs? Watch the ads in women's magazines.

Salvage stores. You never know what you will find in a salvage store but if you live near enough to one to make a once-a-month excursion, you will eventually find what you need with the exception of such things as coats and suits.

Salvage stores get their wares from various places, some of the most common being railroads and truck lines. What happens is that part of a shipment is damaged and an insurance company has to pay the claim. In order to recoup part of its losses the insurance company sells the merchandise to a salvage store.

Time Is Money

If Only . . .

All of us say, "I'd really like to __________ (your choice) if only I could find the time."

Your fill-in for that blank may have been such things as, "I'd really like to sky-dive or learn to speak Spanish or serve as a Pink Lady at the hospital if only I could find the time." Regardless of what your fill-in may have been it shows one thing. None of us ever think we have enough time for the things we want to do. I can imagine that on the last day of Methuselah's nine hundred sixty-ninth year he still had an unfinished list of things he would like to do as soon as he had the time!

People like to explain that they do not have time particularly when it comes to saving money: "I don't have time to go to more than one grocery store." "I don't have time to cook from scratch." "I don't have time to shop the clearance sales." None of us *have* time for these chores; we must *make* time!

In Bible times homemaking was more time-consuming than it is now, yet the women of those days found time to shop daily. Without canned and frozen foods to rely upon, food buying was a daily task. If those homemakers, without benefit of refrigerators, automobiles, and cake mixes managed to find time to shop, doesn't it seem a bit ridiculous for today's homemaker to do less?

I would not be honest if I told you that it takes only a few minutes to bargain hunt. Being a dedicated bargain hunter and a competent money manager takes time and a great deal of effort. It *is* faster to walk into the grocery store with no list and snatch what catches your eye. It *is* faster to buy your daughter a new coat rather than to remodel her sister's outgrown one.

Most of us somehow manage to find time for the things which interest us. The man who loves golf is going to play golf even if his front lawn doesn't get mowed. The woman who loves getting her hair done is going to the beauty shop even if she has to leave her bed unmade to get to her appointment on time. *All of us make time for what we truly want to do.*

If staying home with your children means more to you than taking an outside job, you are going to find a way to do it. If penny-pinching is what it takes to accomplish that goal, then you will find time to do it.

Perhaps it is a mistake to talk of "finding" time because this implies that great chunks of time are lying hidden from view like Easter eggs hidden for the traditional egg hunt. It is better to say we will "make" time. This implies a diligent creative effort on the part of the person making the schedule.

Let us look at some of the ways homemakers can make more time for bargain hunting activities:

"A Place for Everything . . ."

Any time you have to search for an item you need, you are wasting time and eventually money. Since the amount of time allotted to us all is only twenty-four hours a day, the time you lose by being disorganized is going to take time from another activity. Thus, because bargain hunting seems to be a more expendable activity than sleeping, eating, or maybe even watching television, bargain hunting is going to be the activity that gets shoved aside.

A saying goes, "It takes money to make money," and in the case of making time for bargain hunting this axiom is certainly true. You may have to spend a few dollars to get yourself better organized, but if the end result is more time for comparison shopping you will have made a wise investment.

If you haven't toured a hardware store or a building supply warehouse lately, try it. You will be amazed at the plethora of items designed to make your life less cluttered. Does your ironing board fall out of the closet each time the closet door is opened? For a few dollars you can buy a wall-mounted ironing board holder that has a space for the iron as well as the board. Are you short of space for storing canned goods. Buy a wire shelf arrangement which holds about a hundred cans to fasten to the door of a closet. Can you never find a pencil and pad when you use your wall telephone? You may buy a handy contraption which fits around your wall phone to hold these items neatly.

These are just a few of the things that can help make your life orderly and can give you more time for the kind of shopping which will leave extra dollars in your pocket. Look around your own house. Do you see clutter which could be eliminated in order to give you more available time?

Getting Organized

Large corporations hire motion study engineers to carefully observe each motion taken by the workers. The engineers then plan the most efficient placement of people and materials to minimize the time wasted.

You may not be able to afford your own expert, but you can apply the same principles in your work. Observe your wasted motions and unnecessary steps. Experiment with new methods of doing things. Watch your friends fold towels, wash dishes, or dust the furniture and if their method is faster, be flexible enough to change your ways.

Learn to look for the less than obvious means of saving time. Are you changing the bed linen once a week? Would changing it every eight days work as well? If so, you will cut your linen changing time from fifty-two to forty-one times a year without sacrificing much cleanliness. This sets off a chain reaction. If you have two beds to change and two sets of linen make a washerload of dirty clothes, the new procedure will cut your washing by eleven loads a year, which in turn will cut your laundry folding and putting away time.

The best means of saving time is to eliminate some of the jobs you are doing. Of course, this is something that only you can decide. Just because I don't iron sheets does not mean you will want to give up the practice. Some things which are important to you should be continued even if other people think those actions are useless. You can search for other ways to save time.

One of the reasons for a great deal of wasted motion is badly placed tools. Keep your scissors in the sewing basket and buy the children a separate pair for their projects. Get extra trash cans so that you don't have to walk all over the house to dispose of a piece of junk mail. If you have a two-story house, keep cleaning supplies on both floors. Wasted steps cost time and money.

How to Do Two Things at Once

Whoever said you can only do one thing at a time obviously never tried keeping house. Of course, we homemakers can do several things simultaneously! If you haven't learned the trick you are missing one of the best time-saving secrets of all. While a load of wash is chugging away, I start breakfast. While the bacon is cooking, I pack lunches. By the time breakfast is ready the lunches are done and so is the wash.

You can hem a skirt while you talk on the telephone or have a mother-daughter talk while one washes dishes and the other dries. Save your sitting down tasks requiring little concentration and utilize the formerly wasted television time. I fold laundry, shell pecans, make quilts, sew, tear recipes out of magazines, and write letters while I am enjoying my family's company and a television program.

Learning to Save Time

We don't want to become so routine bound that we take all the pleasure out of life, but a certain amount of routine is necessary to good household management if you want to save the maximum amount of time.

Find out what routine works for you by experimenting. Only you can work out a program to fit your lifestyle. However, here are some things which work well for me:

1. Get moving in the morning. I am not by nature a cheerful, bounce-out-of-bed-with-vigor-and-enthusiasm person early in the morning. I have, however, with diligent practice learned to crawl out of bed when called and to muster a measure of determination to replace the missing vigor and enthusiasm. (I am still working on the cheerful part!) Early rising is the key to a successful day. If, after sending everybody off to school and work you can look about and see that the wash is done, the beds made, the dirty dishes gone, and the house clean, you have set the tone for the rest of the day. If you feel defeated in the morning it is hard to rid yourself of the feeling during the rest of the day.

2. Know your own peaks. Everybody has certain times of the day when they are most effective. My peak time is between ten o'clock in the morning and one o'clock in the afternoon, so that is when I schedule my most important work. Define your own peak energy period and use it the same way. Why struggle to wash windows at nine o'clock in the morning if you know you will be having a burst of energy around four o'clock in the afternoon? Doing the hardest jobs during your peak energy times helps you finish your chores much faster.

3. Make lists. Show me an organized person and I will show you a probable list maker. Making lists takes a great deal of the worry out of the chores you have to do, and crossing off a finished chore provides a certain amount of satisfaction. Lists save both time and money. If you have to make a special trip to the Post Office because you forgot to do it while you were out buying bread, taking books to the library, and stopping at the dry cleaners, you have wasted both time and money. A list helps to prevent this occurrence.

4. Do the hard things first. Having the job you hate most behind you gives you a certain edge on the rest of the chores you have to do for the remainder of the day. Thinking all day about a job you despise only prolongs the agony. Do it and get it over with—the same way you used to deal with the castor oil your mother made you take!

5. Trim the fat. Some chores which take up a great deal of time cannot be eliminated, but, by careful planning, the time consuming elements can be modified. For instance, for a number of years I wore my hair quite long. This required setting it and spending time sitting under a hair dryer. By changing to a short, blow-dry style, I saved several hours of time each week.

6. Restructure your lifestyle. Curing yourself of "telephonitus" is difficult, but if you are spending hours each week with your ear glued to the telephone, changing this habit can drastically increase the amount of time you have available for comparison shopping. Likewise, unplug the television if you can't resist it.

7. Do things little by little. If a job can be broken into several steps it is sometimes easier to conquer than by doing it in one sweep. Clean one shelf instead of tearing apart everything in the kitchen. There will be another day when you have a spare fifteen minutes to clean another shelf.

8. Save steps when possible. When going from one room to another look around to see if anything can be taken with you. Make one trip serve more than one purpose. After emptying trash cans set them by the door. The first person who heads toward the room where the cans belong can take them with him.

9. Eliminate clutter. One of the biggest time wasters is dusting objects which serve no useful purpose. Try rotating your bric-a-brac. Put three-fourths of it away and enjoy what is left for six months. Then put that portion in the attic and take out a different batch. The decorating effect you achieve will be much nicer and your dust cloth will enjoy the vacation. The time you save in dusting will be enough to enable you to study the grocery ads.

10. Plan ahead. Do you have a meeting to attend? Don't fry bacon for breakfast if there is no time to scrub the stove. Make cheese toast or boiled eggs and save yourself an extra step. Will you be called on again this year to supply cupcakes for the school's annual bake sale which will take place on the same day you have a dentist's appointment and while a big sale is scheduled at the outlet store where you shop? Bake the cupcakes ahead of time and freeze them. Do you always seem short of time for such things as washing your hair on Saturday night? Arrange a time when the bathroom is less in demand, such as early on Saturday morning.

13

Does It Pay for Homemakers to Work Outside the Home?

Is It Scriptural?

These are confusing times for women. While for centuries women struggled within the confines imposed by society, the freedom available today is, for many, much more confusing than the old traditions ever were. No longer do we suffer from a lack of options. We now have too many of them.

In spite of the trend toward careers outside the home, many women are refusing to take outside jobs because they realize the major advantage of the new freedom: homemaking is no longer a "have to" career. Many women are expressing their preference for staying at home in order to raise their children as they see best.

Many Christians wonder if the woman who works is doing the wrong thing. Yet the Bible cites several instances of women who had careers other than homemaking. Deborah was a judge of Israel. Lydia was a businesswoman who sold purple dye. Priscilla worked alongside her husband as a tent-maker.

Perhaps the most dramatic example of model womanhood is offered in the last chapter of Proverbs. Here is the picture of the dedicated homemaker who is proficient in all areas of her chosen career. She makes a good breakfast for her family (v. 15), gardens (v. 16), finds time to sew (v. 22), engages in charity (v. 20), and teaches her children well (v. 26). The surprising thing about this virtuous woman is that she is more than a homemaker. She has her own thriving home business, too: "She maketh fine linen, and selleth it; and she delivereth girdles unto the merchant" (Prov. 31:24).

The question, then, is not whether a woman can work outside her home and still fulfill her Christian duties, but whether she can make such an undertaking pay.

Can You Afford to Work?

Frequently tearful women have told me, "I don't want to leave my children, but I have to go to work." My reply to that statement is, "Are you sure you can afford to work?"

It costs money to work outside your home. Yet when a family is financially pinched it seems there are only two solutions. Either the husband must take on two jobs or the wife must go to work. However, the problem is not that simple. Most women, particularly those who find part-time jobs, do not make as high an hourly wage as most men do. Therefore, the discouraged job-hunting wife who is perfectly willing to take a job so that her husband will not have to moonlight, may find to her dismay that her husband can make more money with a part-time job than she can with a full-time job. But a lower income is not her only problem. If the children are young she has child care to consider. There is also the matter of transportation and new clothes. It costs money to work and often what it costs is more than the average family can afford. Therefore, for most families, the wife's job is not profitable. It may give her enjoyment, mental stimulation, and a better outlook on life, but it won't give her much money unless she is well educated. Even then, a few years absence from the job market will have taken a toll on her job skills.

What Does It Cost?

The woman seriously considering taking a job to supplement the family income should first sit down and itemize the expenditures to be dealt with if she does find outside employment. First, write down the weekly pay you expect to receive. Now divide that by fifty to determine the true hourly pay rate. Of course, you will be working forty hours per week, not fifty, but consider how long you will be gone from home each week in order to work those forty hours. Will you have an hour for lunch? If so, your forty-hour week has just become forty-five hours. Will it take a half hour to drive to work and a half hour to drive home? If so, your forty-five hours have just been increased to fifty hours away from home each week. The total amount of time involved in the job is the time factor which must be used in estimating the job's financial worth.

The second item on the list is deductions. Regardless of how small your pay, employers are required to deduct for taxes and Social Security. When you are told what your salary is to be, ask about the deductions. Knowing what your take-home pay is going to be will allow you to make a more accurate decision about the feasibility of taking the job.

The next consideration is the cost. What are you going to be required to spend in order to bring that paycheck home? Write down your estimates for such things as transportation, lunches, and parking fees. Also, check to see if you will be paying union dues or if you will be asked to contribute to the company's favorite charity. Then make an estimate of such things as increased wear and tear on your car as well as the extra tires, insurance, and so on you will need. Now consider your wardrobe. If you have been staying home for a number of years and living in casual clothes, going to work may bring you the expense of a complete new wardrobe.

The next factor is convenience. Since you will be away from home fifty hours a week, will it be necessary to change your family's eating style? Will you be using more convenience foods or going out to eat more frequently? Will you need to update your kitchen equipment if you go out to work? Since time is a critical factor for the career woman you may need to add new items such as a food processor, a microwave oven, a slow cooker, or any other time-saving gadget you don't already own.

After all these things have been considered, add up the total and subtract this from the amount of pay you are expecting. Quite likely, the total won't be appealing, because after all the necessities are subtracted and divided by the fifty hours away from home each week, what is left may be far less than the minimum hourly wage. What makes this picture even more dismal is that for the woman without a high school diploma or job experience, the minimum hourly wage may have been the starting point.

What Must I Give Up in Order to Work?

That small figure left after you make all those subtractions is still not the net amount you will make from your job.

What do you suppose your bargain hunting is worth? Let's think just of the bargains you are able to get by comparison shopping in the three grocery stores you go into each week. Working women don't have that amount of time to spend. Most manage to go to only one store.

Try this experiment before deciding that what you would lose by giving up grocery bargain hunting is worthwhile. Go into one of the stores where you normally shop and calculate what it would cost to buy all the items on your grocery list. Then buy what you need and proceed with the remainder of your shopping in the other stores you usually frequent. Afterwards, compare the "what if I had shopped in only one store" total with the actual total you spent. Most likely, the results will astonish you. Unbelievable as it may seem the extra amount you will spend by giving up bargain hunting may be as much as three meals normally cost.

Try another experiment. Go into the grocery store after five o'clock on Friday or anytime during the day on Saturday. You will notice that it is much more difficult to do the mental arithmetic you need to do because of the crowd of jostling customers. Also, many of the advertised specials will be gone. After spending twice as much shopping time as you normally spend you will be in a better position to realistically evaluate whether you are willing to undertake this kind of effort each week if you do choose to go to work.

How about all the other bargain hunting you do? Working women miss a great many bargains because they can't be at the shopping center when it opens in the morning. Also, some specialty stores aren't open at convenient hours for working women. Then, too, taking fifty hours out of your week automatically cuts down on the time available for bargain hunting. Are you willing to give up the several hundred dollars you can save by being a bargain hunter?

There is also the matter of doing things yourself. If you go to work will it be necessary to hire someone to paint your kitchen or mow your lawn? All of these things you no longer have time for will subtract from your new salary.

How about the garden you grow? Will you still have time to sow, cultivate, can, and freeze? If not, this will be a loss of up to five hundred dollars in grocery money each year. How about all the new clothes you make for your family? Will you find yourself paying twice as much for each garment as it would have cost had you found time to make it yourself?

What do you do about Christmas gifts? While Christmas traditionally is a time of considerable spending, the homemaker who can make stuffed animals, homemade cookies, ceramics, and crocheted stoles comes out ahead of the homemaker who, because of her limited time, must buy all her gifts ready made. Depending on your family's way of spending money during the Christmas season, this loss of time could result in a spending increase of several hundred dollars each December.

It might seem a bit time consuming to calculate all these costs, but this is the only way you can get a realistic view of whether it would be worthwhile financially to take a job. Once, as part of my research for a magazine article I was writing on whether women can afford to work, I did this same kind of calculating. After going to several prospective employers, applying, and discussing starting salaries, I had a reasonably realistic figure with which to work. A friend who was a payroll clerk supplied me with the figures for state and federal taxes and Social Security deductions. From there I figured my expenses as I have asked you to figure yours. The result was that if I had decided to work outside my home my net pay would have been $187. That doesn't sound bad for a week's work, does it? The only problem was that this amount was not for a week or even a month. It was the amount I would clear in *a whole year of working!*

Are you wondering if I took any of those jobs for which I had applied? Absolutely not! I can't afford to work outside my home!

Homemaking as a Career

Here are some alternatives to taking an outside job:

1. Realize that homemaking is a career, too. Quite often I have heard women say things such as, "I'm trying to decide whether I want to be a homemaker or whether I want a career." But homemaking *can* be a career. Too many women see homemaking only as a way of marking time and even if their motives are noble—"It's my duty to stay home and be a full-time mother while the children are little"—the results are not spectacular. Only when a woman sees her job as a homemaker as a worthwhile and rewarding career can she truly make it pay.

Yes, homemaking can *pay*. It's just that the monetary rewards of homemaking may not be so glaringly obvious. First, see that homemaking is just as much a career as teaching school, typing letters, or laying bricks. Then apply your intelligence and skills toward making that career show the most possible dividends. Learn to shop intelligently. Learn to do things yourself. Learn to be the most economical cook on the block.

Homemaking will not be boring if every skill you possess is employed. Any training you already have whether you were educated to be a teacher, accountant, bank clerk, or waitress, can in some way be utilized to improve your homemaking skills. All those jobs required discipline and were at times boring just as homemaking requires discipline and will at times be boring. When you stop seeing homemaking as a job and start seeing it as a career you will make strides toward making monetary gains from your profession.

2. Learn and use shopping skills. Take the time to learn to recognize good buys and to know how to comparison shop. Each dollar you save is a dollar you don't have to earn in the job marketplace.

3. Use your skills creatively. Experiment with new ways to cut costs. As a full-time homemaker you have the luxury of doing just that. Think of cost-cutters which involve time rather than money. Making your own Christmas gifts is an example of this.

4. Be a do-it-yourselfer. Whatever it is that you need to learn to do, chances are your public library has a book on that subject. Ask around and you may discover a friend who can offer some expert advice. Everything you can learn to do for yourself leaves money available in your budget for other purposes. Don't be timid about trying new projects and don't limit yourself to narrow concepts of what constitutes women's work. If you are good at refinishing old furniture or putting up storm windows there is no reason you shouldn't do these things. Maybe your husband will swap a job he hates for one you have been doing and both of you can get an extra benefit from the do-it-yourself program.

14

Finding More Money to Manage

Adding to the Family Budget

Many women become full-time homemakers because of an "ought-to" attitude, rather than a "want-to" attitude. Some even stay at home full-time because of an idea that making money is strictly the husband's obligation.

As the head of the household, the husband is charged to provide for the financial as well as the spiritual needs of the family: "But if any provide not for his own, and specially for those of his own house, he hath denied the faith, and is worse than an infidel" (I Tim. 5:8). But it does not appear to be scripturally forbidden for the wife to cooperate in this endeavor.

As was noted in Chapter Thirteen, it does not pay for the average wife with small children to work. The word *average*, however, is becoming quite difficult to define. Because of changes in our culture it is not always possible to spot that hypothetically average family which consists of a father, a mother, and two children. Instead, households may contain more than one generation, may contain several unrelated families, or be headed by a woman instead of a man. Divorce or death of the husband has left many women without the option of whether they will work outside the home. If there is no other breadwinner, these women scarcely have an option. However, it seems that even these women who work because they must, feel somewhat negligent in their duties because of their inability to stay at home with their children.

How does the Bible see working women? No Scripture forbids women to work. Instead, we have the example set by a number of women who, while holding down a full-time job, still found time to attend to their spiritual duties as well.

Deborah was a judge of Israel, yet she was a married woman. Her job was one of great responsibility since it involved not only a great deal of time spent in person-to-person counseling, but also a knowledge of military strategy (Judg. 4). Priscilla was a notable woman of the New Testament. She worked alongside her husband at their profession of tent-making (Acts 18:2). Lydia was a wealthy woman whose wealth came from her own successful business. She was a seller of purple dye (Acts 16:14).

The significant thing about each of these women is not that she had a career outside her home, but that she had the ability to schedule her employment in such a way as to leave time for spiritual matters as well.

It must, however, also be noted that no mention is made of whether any of these women had children. This may be the key to the whole matter of taking an outside job. Women *do* have an obligation to their families. Paul urged that the older women set an example for the younger ones, "That they may teach the young women to be sober, to love their husbands, to love their children, to be discreet, chaste, keepers at home, good, obedient to their own husbands, that the word of God be not blasphemed" (Titus 2:5-6).

The Christian mother who cannot make her budget work out unless she adds additional funds feels caught in the middle. She wants to see her children brought up properly but must have more household money in order to care for their physical requirements. Is there a solution?

For many women the answer is found in two directions. First, by becoming the best possible steward of the funds at her disposal, a homemaker can decrease her need for additional household money. Then, if this tactic alone is not sufficient there is another alternative to taking a job. As I detailed in my book *Money in the Cookie Jar*, numerous homemakers are devising ways to make money without leaving home. Whether by babysitting occasionally, creating handicrafts for the consignment shop, or collecting recyclable cans or papers, these enterprising women are successfully adding dollars to the family budget *without going out to work*.

Proverbs 31:10-31 offers a role model for women who wish to strive toward the epitome of ideal womanhood. Various aspects of homemaking are discussed in these verses, but two things in particular are significant for the mother whose budget is not sufficient. Unlike the other working women of the Bible, this composite of the ideal woman is clearly shown as a mother (v. 28). Yet among the many duties this woman found time to excel in she managed to bring in extra cash. This woman had a profitable home business: "She maketh fine linen, and selleth it; and delivereth girdles unto the merchant" (v. 24).

Making money without taking an outside job can be done in numerous ways, such as swapping goods or services, selling a service or a product, utilizing creative ideas, or dealing with recyclables.

The Creative Money Maker

Have you ever found yourself in a pressing financial bind and, in order to meet an immediate need, you held a garage sale? That is a typical example of how creative money-making works. While many women neither need or want a permanent job, nor even a flexible one such as a home business, most of us at times need some sudden cash.

The unique quality possessed by the creative money maker is her ability to see "right now" opportunities. She doesn't spend a great deal of time moaning over her lack of funds. Instead, she sees an opportunity and takes advantage of it immediately.

A garage sale offers the perfect opportunity for this kind of person. It doesn't tie her down indefinitely yet supplies her with the funds she needs temporarily. Splendid though the garage sale idea is, it is usually a one time operation. Everybody runs out of junk eventually. If that is the case with you, here are some additional ideas you might want to try for those occasional times when you want a quick money-making plan:

1. Find a salable freebie. A member of my husband's family moved into a house with a yard full of pecan trees. When tax time came she wondered how she would pay the bill. Then, looking out her window she saw the answer. After a few days spent collecting and selling pecans she acquired the cash she needed for the tax payment.

Look around to see if you have similar items you could collect and sell. If not, look further. Many people like wild plums, blackberries, and various kinds of nuts but they don't want to take the time to pick them. Even if you don't have any edibles on your own property, you may be able to locate someone willing to let you go into his woods and harvest what you want. One of my friends who lies in the north Georgia mountains makes a tidy sum each year from the sale of gallons of blackberries she picks and sells. If you live near the ocean, you might want to consider gathering and selling clams. Anytime you go on someone else's property be sure to get permission first, even if the property is only a stretch of woods or beach.

If you have a talent for recognizing wild herbs, this is a salable commodity, too. Many exclusive restaurants prefer fresh herbs when they can get them. Likewise, the gathering of plants and flowers which can be used in dried arrangements can be a profitable undertaking. Just be sure you are selecting only those plants which are not endangered species and can be gathered without harm to you.

Look around your neighborhood to see what kinds of businesses are located there. There is no need to spend hours gathering something only to discover that you have no market for it. An item which might sell in certain areas won't sell at all in others.

An Alabama friend occasionally makes a little spending money by collecting certain wild grasses used by a local factory to make skin ointment. Another friend in Hawaii adds to his spare spending money by locating certain kinds of shells which dealers want. There is no end to what can be gathered and sold. Find out what is in demand in your area.

Of course, some freebies you gather will need a bit of attention before being sold. The local florist might be more interested in your pine cones if you agree to snip them into the flat "roses" which are often used in dried arrangements. The wild plums you gathered might be more salable if converted into homemade plum jelly. The nuts you collect might be more appealing if you offer them shelled.

The creative money maker can also make extra funds by recognizing an opportunity when it unexpectedly arises. She has the ability to see a need and to fill it quickly. When a friend complains that the baby sitter didn't arrive or that the boy who mows the lawn is moving, the creative money maker offers more than sympathy. Any skill or knowledge she possesses can be called upon at a moment's notice when a money-making opportunity appears.

While you might not want the responsibility of a regular home business, any skill suitable for such a purpose is also suitable for occasional money-making opportunities. Let it be known that you will sew, fill out income tax returns, or walk the dog for friends who find themselves in an occasional predicament.

2. Start a seasonal business. As I pointed out in my book, *Money in the Cookie Jar*, running a home business takes a great deal of time and effort. If you do it full-time it is as tiring and time consuming as any other job. However, if you aren't ready for this kind of commitment, try having a seasonal home business instead. If you have accounting skills, tax season offers many opportunities. If you have baking skills, Christmas gifts may be paid for with money earned from goods made in your own kitchen. If you have typing skills, a bulletin board ad at the local college may bring you a bundle of term papers at the end of the semester.

A seasonal business can be selected just as a full-time business would be, with the exception that it is done on a limited basis. Two women I met at a craft show confided that they work feverishly from fall through December each year to make elegant wreaths from pine cones and other natural materials. During the rest of the year they are free to pursue other interests. A home business doesn't have to be a permanent thing. The whole idea is to make some money in a way that does not disrupt your lifestyle.

3. ***Learn to swap and trade.*** Money is not the only payment you can receive for your services and products. I once sewed for a woman who paid me with crocheted jewelry which I used as Christmas gifts. Another time I babysat for a couple and, since the father worked in a meat market, I was paid in steaks rather than in dollars.

Bartering is a good, old-fashioned way of doing business. If you ever swapped a book or a bag of marbles during your childhood, you have engaged in barter. If so, you know that such an exchange can be much more interesting than the exchange of cash. Be certain to give the person you are exchanging with full value of the swap while making certain you get full value, too. Don't swap such things as coins, antiques, glassware, and collectibles unless you are knowledgeable about such things.

The things you can barter are limited only by your imagination. Any goods you own or can produce as well as any service you can perform are good opportunities for barter.

4. ***Collect recyclables.*** With the interest in ecology which has developed in recent years, manufacturers have been more or less forced to make an effort at recycling. Therefore,

if you live near a reasonably large city you can probably find a market for such things as aluminum cans and old newspapers.

The problem is that in most cases the buyers of such items are not interested unless you have a large amount of the product. With newspaper dealers, a hundred pounds is about the minimum amount they are interested in buying. Consequently, unless you can get into recycling in a concentrated manner, this sort of business is not going to work. Your own pile of newspapers won't grow that rapidly. You can, however, obtain paper in other ways. Some libraries throw out surplus papers. It would do no harm to ask your librarian about this. If you have a friend or relative in data processing ask to acquire the thrown away print-outs. These are salable once the carbon is removed and since this paper is heavier than newsprint the profit mounts quickly. The paper also stores tidily. Many dealers will take old telephone books. If you live in an area where the phone books are quite hefty—perhaps as much as five pounds a set—investigate the possibility of collecting other people's discarded phone books. Find out when new books are delivered and follow the route the delivery person makes.

Another possibility is corrugated cardboard. However, this is more difficult to deal with than is paper. The cardboard must be flattened and tied with string, and a truck is needed to transport it. If, however, you have access to both a truck and a source of cardboard you might want to give this a try. Your best source of cardboard is not your average grocery store. Try instead one of the economy stores where no grocery sacks are used. Since these stores display goods in boxes which have had the tops cut off, they may be willing to let you have the flat pieces which cannot be used for other purposes. To find a dealer for your cardboard, look in the yellow pages of your telephone book under "Waste Paper" or "Recyclable Products."

Aluminum cans are another source of potential income. Look for soft-drink machines with large trash cans nearby. If the proprietor is not interested in recycling the cans himself, he may agree to let you haul away the cans for him. The cans must be clean inside and out and must be smashed flat before taking them to a recycling center. To find a dealer, look under "Recyclable Products" in the yellow pages of your phone book.

Many other things such as the lead in old batteries and the aluminum parts from old cars and refrigerators can also be sold, but generally such things as cans, cardboard, and newspapers are what most of us have access to. If you have a family business which has a surplus of one kind of waste or another, by all means check with the recycling centers.

5. *Get involved with refunding.* Manufacturers hope to convince consumers to develop product loyalty, but in order to accomplish this goal they must first convince the potential customer to buy. They do this by offering money back for buying certain products. There is no "catch" to refunding as some people believe. See Chapter Five for more on refunding.

15

Children and Money

The Scriptural Basis for Childhood Training

"Train up a child in the way he should go: and when he is old he will not depart from it" (Prov. 22:6).

While this verse is generally taken to mean that parents should see to the spiritual training of their children it goes far beyond that. Parents are responsible for *all* aspects of their children's preparation for adulthood. Even money management must be taught by the parents, because if it is not taught the child will grow to become a financially irresponsible adult.

Many Christian parents do their children a great disservice by failing to teach them proper principles of money management. Inevitably the parent who neglects this is going to suffer for his lack of instruction. Look around at some of the Christian families you know. You probably know at least one with a physically adult child who has never grown into a responsible adult capable of handling his own money affairs. Perhaps you know a thirty-year-old who still thinks it is Mother and Daddy's responsibility to pay his car insurance, his wife's doctor bills, or his children's school fees. That clinging offspring didn't become that way overnight. His behavior resulted from a gradual molding process by his loving and well-meaning parents.

What does proper child rearing have to do with your own effective money management? Everything! Only by enlisting the aid of every member of your family can your budget work successfully. No matter how young your children are they should be hearing financial discussions. It is hard to make a budget work when a child is screaming for a new ten-speed bike. By making that child a part of your money management program you won't have to tell him no when something is beyond your means. He will already understand what is being done with "all that money Daddy brings home" and he will see that he will have to forget the new bike or work with you on the budget to make the purchase possible.

Many Bible scholars have speculated that Jesus worked as a carpenter in Joseph's shop. In former days children were expected to work. Childhood was not a carefree time spent doing only things that were enjoyable. By the time a Hebrew boy was thirteen years old he was considered a man and was expected to work like one.

Even into the twentieth century children were a large part of the work force. Now laws protect children and give them the rights they deserve, but in previous years this was not so. In 1860 my great-great-grandfather employed two young men to do his plowing for him. The ages of those "men"? One was ten years old and the other twelve!

Thankfully things are better now, but in throwing away the bad we have also thrown out a portion of the good. While my child or yours might take a stick of peppermint candy for granted, I'm sure those young plowboys didn't. They knew exactly how long it took to earn that peppermint stick. If children of former times learned money management, can we do less for our own privileged children?

Financial education for children doesn't just happen. It is

the result of concentrated effort on the part of Christian parents. Parents not only must teach, they must also show. Even the attitude toward giving to God must be nurtured and shown by example:

> My son, forget not my law; but let thine heart keep my commandments (Prov. 3:1).
>
> Honour the Lord with thy substance, and with the firstfruits of all thine increase (Prov. 3:9).
>
> Hear, ye children, the instruction of a father, and attend to know understanding (Prov. 4:1).

Teaching by Example

Children, even young ones, are much more clever than adults may think. Children can see right through the "do as I say, not as I do" system of teaching. That is why it is so vital for parents to show as well as tell their children about money management.

How can you show your child proper money management? First, bring him into family discussions about finances. A five-year-old isn't likely to come up with any fantastic methods of cutting household expense, but by asking, "What do you think we could do to keep from spending as much money as we do on the light bill?" you raise his awareness of the problem while giving him a chance to see that he is part of the team. Building self-confidence in a child contributes to his desire to learn. The fact that the family takes time to listen to his ideas is going to make your five-year-old eager to look for additional ideas to discuss. At first his motive may be to gain attention but after a while his attitude toward money begins to form. Showing him that his opinion and cooperation counts is more beneficial than a lecture on money management after he reaches his teen years.

The second way to teach is through consistency. If you are against charge cards one month and in favor of them the next, your child is going to see money management as a silly game. If you cut corners one month and splurge heedlessly the next he is not going to take your budget discussions seriously.

Another vital point is to show your Christian commitment. A four-year-old isn't being a smart aleck when he asks why he must put his money in the Sunday school collection instead of spending it on an ice cream cone. He is going through the process of sorting out his mental attitudes about money. His biggest boost toward learning about tithing is the example you set. If you use your tithes to buy a new dress one week, he is not going to believe what you tell him about stewardship the next week. Only by showing by example that giving to God makes you happier than buying a new dress can you convince him that he did the right thing in giving up that ice cream cone.

Helping a Child to See

A child has to participate in order to learn. All the theory in the world won't take the place of a few intelligent discussions or informative shopping trips.

When my daughter Karen was a preschooler we discussed the fact that all the commercials on a morning television program consisted of sales pitches for cereal or toys. Later as we watched the evening news we noted that such things as automobiles, snack foods, and products for adult consumers were advertised. It wasn't long before Karen observed, "Those people who pay for television programs just want us to buy what they make, don't they?" After we had talked about this for a while she began to notice how advertised goods looked much more wonderful on television than in real life. After comparing the toys in the commercials with some of the toys in her own toy box, she acquired enough cynicism about advertising to be a wary consumer, even at five.

Later, after she had learned to read, I noticed that each time we went to the store, instead of asking for the advertised cereals she would pick up a box, read the ingredients label, and quietly put it back on the shelf. When I questioned her actions she told me, "I'm checking to see if sugar is listed as the first or second ingredient. That's the way you do it, isn't it?"

Admittedly, the shopping goes faster if you go alone, and with small children it is difficult to do the necessary arithmetic to figure out which brand is the better bargain. However, once the child is old enough to understand what you are talking about he should be allowed to accompany you on at least some of your shopping trips. If you have several children try taking one at a time so you can give undivided consumer lessons to each.

The important thing is not to lay down rules, but to allow them to learn for themselves what a bargain is. By the time they are eight or nine years old they can be counted on to spot bargains you may not have noticed.

Explain as you go along. Let them know why the washable coat is a better value than a similar priced coat with a dry clean label. Show them the bruises on some of the apples and ask them to help you find better ones.

Allowances

There are about as many opinions on allowances as there are parents to hold those opinions. Some say it is easier to work on a "cash as he needs it" basis while others rely on an inflexible amount that is doled out to each child regardless of age.

Allowances can be a trial when a child is young and does not fully understand the principles involved, but allowances still seem to be the best method of teaching a child good principles of money management. A child shouldn't have to beg or plead for each quarter but should have money of his own. Having him ask for his spending money teaches him to rely on a winning smile or a quick hug as means of manipulating.

How much allowance should a child get? There is no one answer to that question. It depends on various factors, including the age of the child, the responsibility of the child, and your expectations regarding what he is to do with the money.

Allowances should come with no strings attached. It is not a payment for good behavior nor is it a bribe to assure the parents freedom from endless begging. It is the child's portion of the family income.

When Karen was three we began giving her an allowance of fifty cents a week. We sat down with her and discussed the responsibilities of so vast a sum and showed her how she could have a tithe envelope just as we did. We discussed various ways to handle the money, including saving part of it or spending it on snacks or toys. Of course, she made mistakes with it and even lost it once or twice, but the important thing was the learning process. Her food and clothing were supplied by us, but she was responsible for extras such as coloring books and bubble liquid. Soon she was picking out two or three coloring books she liked, asking the price of each and then making her final decision based on the lowest price. Giving her an allowance had taught her money management principles no lecture could have conveyed.

As my daughter gets older we increase both her allowance and the responsibilities that go with it. Now, not only is the money for fun items, but for certain bills of her own. Out of her funds she buys her own school supplies, contributes to our church mission fund, gives her tithe, pays for gifts, and takes care of her own ticket when she goes skating. Of course, with each new category added to her responsibility it is necessary to raise the total allowance so that she can take care of her obligations and still have something left over for herself. As she grows the allowance will be increased as will the responsibilities that go with it, so that by the time she is fourteen she will be budgeting her own clothing expenses.

By now some of you may be thinking, "Well, that works for your daughter, but my child would never do that. He would spend the whole thing on candy and would never have anything left." At first many children will do such things. However, if you give him an adequate amount and refuse to give him any more until the next allowance day he eventually will learn. The child who misses a much wanted excursion with his friends because he handled his money poorly will learn a valuable lesson that will aid him through adulthood. Be persistent and firm and don't bail him out of his financial disasters. If you keep on bailing him out now, you may find yourself doing the same thing when he is forty-five years old and in a never-ending financial jam.

Guiding in the Right Path

Not one woman exists who always handles her money in the best way. All of us make money management mistakes at one time or another and that too is part of the learning process. Rather than hide your mistakes from your children let them know about them. Seeing that you conscientiously strive to overcome the bad judgments you have made is an encouragement to the child who doesn't quite comprehend how he can ever be as perfect in managing his money as he thinks you are in managing yours.

Above all else, teach your children that money cannot buy love, happiness, success, or entrance into eternal life. Money is not the answer to every problem and the child who learns this early in life will be spared a great deal of trouble in later years.

Being a Christian does not insure earthly riches. It is wrong to teach a child that if he tithes he will become wealthy. Teach him instead that using his money in a way that pleases God will bring him contentment whether it brings earthly riches or not. Scripture says, "Better is a dry morsel, and quietness therewith, than an house full of sacrifices with strife" (Prov. 17:1).

Let him be part of the decision-making force regarding finances. When there is not enough money for all the things the family wants, involve the children in working out ways to get the extra funds. Challenge them to help you cut the grocery and electric bill in order to gain the funds for the badminton set they want so badly. They learn the art of money management because you have given them part of the responsibility.

Encourage children to save money. Certainly, in these days of inflation, savings accounts are not the most profitable way of accumulating funds, but for a child the experience of learning to anticipate and save toward future needs is more valuable than the small amount of interest they will earn.

16

Living on a Fixed Income

The Reality of a Lowered Income

In this country, thirty-five million people, or one-sixth of the population, receive monthly Social Security checks. With a 103 billion dollar payroll being used to pay these Social Security recipients the per person average comes out to slightly less than three hundred dollars a month. Obviously, this income is not sufficient to live on.

Yet, millions *do* live on this amount—and less. This amount is only an average. Some recipients get a bit more and vast numbers of them get only one-half to one-third that amount. Learning to use their income efficiently is not for these people merely an interesting diversion, it is a grim matter of survival.

Another 12.5 million people receive military retirement and military disability checks each month. While these checks may represent more than the amounts Social Security recipients get, both groups have one thing in common: Each must learn to live on a fixed amount. There are no Christmas bonuses, no overtime pay, and no profit-sharing plans. These people do get cost-of-living raises, but these don't put them ahead; they just allow them to stay relatively even with inflation.

Too many Americans with fixed incomes are not aware of all the cost-cutting measures which would allow them to improve their standard of living. Others don't have the health or the transportation needed to do the kind of bargain hunting that would help them stretch their dollars. Still others hesitate to accept the discounts and free goods offered to them because they see such things as charity.

There is, however, absolutely nothing wrong in accepting that to which you are entitled. Those who have worked for years and contributed to the retirement fund have a right to enjoy the fruits of their labors in their older years. The discounts and free services offered by many organizations are not charity, but a means of saying "thank you" to citizens who have made worthwhile contributions to their society.

In Bible times there were no such organized advantages as are offered today. The elderly and the disabled were cared for by their families or church. Paul, in writing to Timothy, clearly defined the responsibilities of Christians regarding those in need: "If any man or woman that believeth have widows, let them relieve them, and let not the church be charged; that it may relieve them that are widows indeed" (I Tim. 5:16).

Sources of Help

One of the best ways for the Social Security recipient to stretch her dollars to the maximum is by becoming aware of all the savings possibilities which are available to those over sixty-five and, in some cases, to those over fifty-five.

Merchants frequently give discounts to those over sixty-five and most of the merchants who do this display some sort of notice to this effect. Some restaurants make a practice of deducting 10 percent off the bill of older persons. Others give discount cards to senior citizens. Each time the diner pays his check he simply presents his card and is given the discount.

Banks, too, offer helpful services. Many offer free checking accounts and free checks to anyone over sixty-five. Some banks even provide free photocopying privileges. This in itself is a worthwhile service since many older people are required to make numerous copies of such things as doctor bills and insurance claims. Services vary from bank to bank, so check with more than one before opening your account. Only one in a married couple need be sixty-five in order for both to receive these banking services.

Have you ever wished you could afford to go back to school? If you are sixty-five or older that wish may become reality without any cost to you. In some communities the adult education courses offered by local colleges are available free of charge to senior citizens. Ask, too, about special cost breaks for college credit courses.

One of the most usable of the benefits offered to older people is the discount given by certain drug stores. The usual procedure is to fill out a card containing the necessary information after which you can receive your discount by showing your card at the time of purchase.

Do you find it necessary to have such things as your blood pressure checked frequently? If so, the cost of a doctor visit can be avoided by visiting the Public Health Center in your community. In most cases blood pressure checks are free of charge.

If you like to travel, check into the discounts offered by various motel chains. Some of them offer a club plan whereby older members can receive discounts and other benefits.

If you are at least sixty-two you are eligible for a discount when using certain areas administered by the National Park Service. Contact the National Park Service in Washington, D.C., to obtain your Golden Age Passport which entitles you to a 50 percent discount ticket. These passports can be used for camping and other activities available at National Parks.

Airlines offer discounts to travelers over sixty-five. Generally, this discount is not publicized, but if you ask when you book your ticket, the discount will be given to you if the airline does participate in this sort of program. Be prepared, however, to show proof of your age when you go to pick up your ticket.

Strength in Numbers

Without a doubt, the most effective means of finding all the discounts and advantages available to you is by joining a club designed specifically for people over the age of fifty-five. Through association with others you can compare notes and learn the places to bargain hunt and to obtain discounts. Frequently, too, these clubs have access to discount coupons which the general public might not know about. For instance, at a recent meeting of the Friendship Club to which my parents belong, tickets for a discount priced meal at a popular restaurant were given out.

Perhaps you have wanted to become part of such a group but didn't know how to locate one. Usually, there is at least one such group in the community and finding it is not difficult. Call your local recreation center or some of the larger churches in your area. Generally, you don't have to be a member of the particular church or affiliated with the denomination to participate. Many will have a brief devotional at the start of the meeting, but a good meal and a chance to socialize is the reason for the club's existence. In some neighborhoods organizations such as the YMCA or a civic group might sponsor such a senior citizen's club.

The best part of being a member of such a club is the opportunity to socialize with others of the same age group, but it offers other benefits. Frequently guest speakers present programs specifically designed for older people and in this way you can broaden your horizons.

Since potluck dinners often are a part of club meetings, membership offers a chance to get out of the house and to share a good meal with others.

If you like to travel, club membership can be beneficial in that way, too. Frequently, your group may take day or even weekend trips. A bus is chartered for the group and, because of the number of participants, they are able to get discount rates on food and lodgings. Most of these mini-vacations are much more economical than would be the same trip if you made it on your own.

Transportation

One of the most difficult things for older people to cope with is the matter of getting from one place to another. In many areas volunteer groups provide transportation to doctors' offices and to the grocery store. If you need this kind of help call local churches, the recreation department, or the county's department of family and children's services. Someone will know where to refer you for the kind of transportation you need.

If you wish to vote on election day and can't drive yourself to the polls, many of the civic organizations will help you get there. Contact the League of Women Voters, city hall, or even the office of the candidate you support.

Staying Informed

One of the best ways to know what benefits are available to you is through contact with others of your age. This can be done through clubs and through reading publications geared to the older American. By staying informed on subjects which affect your lifestyle, you can learn new ways of coping with retirement. Check your local library or bookstore for senior citizen magazines.

A Round-Up of Money-Saving Ideas to Try

- If you enjoy reading, locate a bookstore which specializes in used paperback books. To make your reading dollar go even further, organize about a half-dozen of your friends into a reading club and swap a book at the bookstore only after it has been passed around.
- Check with local wrecking companies for bargain priced building supplies. Such things as doors and mantels are often salvaged and sold. Chandeliers, paneling, mirrors, and antique doorknobs are often offered for sale when old houses are demolished.
- Learn the advantage of auctions. The sheriff's department, the police department, the Post Office department, and the local flea market all hold auctions. If you should happen to encounter a product you need you are likely to get it at a bargain price.
- Turn your kitchen discards into free fertilizer for your garden. Such things as potato peelings, eggshells, tea leaves and coffee grounds are fine for composting. A two-pound

coffee can with a plastic snap-on lid will hold your discards neatly and keep the odor from permeating your kitchen until you accumulate enough material to cart out to the compost pile.

- Read Keith Sehnert's *How to Be Your Own Doctor (Sometimes)* available from Grosset and Dunlap, 51 Madison Avenue, New York, NY 10010. In it, Dr. Sehnert tells how to learn to recognize symptoms and to know whether what you need is on your own medicine shelf or if a doctor visit is necessary.
- Save gasoline by buying postage stamps by the roll and by acquiring a year's worth of birthday and anniversary cards at one time.
- If you think that you have been overcharged by the grocery cashier, bank teller, or the Post Office clerk by all means speak up. At the end of the day their receipts are supposed to match their cash, but many times they have overages which no one claims. In the case of the Post Office you might have to wait two or three months until the stock is audited, but if there is an overage which matches your claimed shortage you will get it.
- Look for barber and beauty colleges if you want real bargains on hair services. While it is a bit risky to allow a novice to cut your hair, a shampoo and set involves relatively little risk and the price will be less than half what you would pay at a salon. During the shampoo-and-set visits observe the students, and if you see one who seems particularly competent you can request her services for a haircut.
- Don't be overly quick to call the repairman when an appliance stops working. First, check for blown fuses and accidental unplugging. An embarrassing number of service calls are paid for by people who never thought to check such things before calling for help.
- Make your own household cleaning products. If you are tired of spending money on high priced cleaning supplies, read *The Formula Book* by Norman Stark. Within its pages you will find exact recipes for everything from oven cleaner

to detergent. (This book is published by Sheed and Ward, Kansas City, Kansas.)

• Buy drugs by generic name rather than by brand name. Ask your doctor to prescribe generic drugs for you so that your pharmacist can fill your prescription in the most economical manner. An example of the meaning of generic is the word "aspirin." Aspirin is the name of the chemical compound, while Bayer and St. Joseph's are brand names for aspirin.

• Familiarize youself with the Post Office's services. Most people waste money by putting too much postage on the items they mail. Learn the rates. The second ounce of a letter's weight does not cost as much as does the first ounce. Books and reading material can be mailed more cheaply than other packages if you specify "educational material." Airgrams cut down on postage rates to foreign countries.

• Some grocery stores sell less than perfect vegetables and extremely ripe fruit by the large bag for practically nothing. Ask the produce managers in the stores where you shop if there is a particular day of the week when you can purchase these goods. You may have to discard quite a bit of the bag's contents but what is left will still be a bargain. A store where I shop charges thirty-nine cents per bag for its imperfect produce. For this price I have bought up to five pounds of green beans, of which about a pound had to be discarded—but that was still a bargain price. I have also bought as many as twenty bell peppers for this price and discarded only five or six. The important thing is to be willing to sort through the produce and to immediately use the bargains you find.

• Radial tires can increase your gasoline mileage. Increasing your tire pressure by four or five pounds per tire can also help. However, exercise caution and do not over-inflate beyond the safe limit.

• Get your children's immunizations at the public health center rather than at the doctor's office. Immunizations are free at the health center.

• Utilize free edibles. Of course, everybody knows about

pecans, wild plums, and clams, but did you also know about poke, escargots, and dandelion greens? Read any of Euell Gibbons' books, such as *Stalking the Wild Asparagus*, to learn more about gathering free edibles. Don't experiment until you are *positive* you know what you are doing.

• Have your legal matters taken care of by a legal clinic. In many cases the cost is about half what you would pay at an individual attorney's office.

• Cut food costs while exploring Chinese cuisine. Such specialties as tofu, soybeans, and bean sprouts furnish protein at a miniscule price. Even main dishes using meat require smaller amounts than American dishes.

• Sewing your own clothing saves money, but you will save even more if you learn to utilize such fabric sources as bargain-priced sheets, pillowcases, and towels. A sheet contains enough fabric to equal three yards of off-the-bolt material and because of its width it goes much further than three yards of regular fabric. One pillowcase makes a toddler a nightgown or a shift. Towels can be used to make sports garments, and with a little imagination cotton tea towels can be transformed into wearables.

• Make your own cosmetics. If you are appalled at the high cost of cosmetics, *The Formula Book* by Norman Stark can help you in that department. To make your creations more appealing, various scents can be ordered from Caswell-Massey. This company carries all the ingredients for perfumery, and what could be more exclusive than creating your own perfume? The address is Caswell-Massey Co. Ltd., 575 Lexington Avenue, New York, NY 10022.

• Some individually owned department stores offer a small discount for customers who pay cash. If you have been wondering about this, ask the manager.

• With the help of ten or twelve other families you can set up a food co-op and get groceries at wholesale prices. However, the co-op will not work unless each member is willing to do her fair share. You must be willing to take turns doing the shopping, bookkeeping, and distribution.

• Get double use from disposables. If you must have disposables, learn to make them go further. Aluminum foil and transparent wrap can be used several times if you carefully wipe them clean with a damp cloth after each use.

- Switch to edible houseplants. Who says a tomato plant isn't just as beautiful as a philodendron? One or two edible houseplants can provide an interesting hobby, a little extra food, and a great stimulant for conversation.
- Learn emergency measures to prevent extra trips to the store. Baking soda can be used as a substitute for toothpaste in a pinch. Just pour a small amount into your hand and dip a wet toothbrush into it. If you are out of window cleaner, vinegar and water works nicely. Tomato soup can be substituted for tomato paste in some recipes. If you are out of baby shampoo apply a streak of petroleum jelly across the baby's forehead to prevent your regular shampoo from running into his eyes.
- Save your leftover bits of soap in a jar. When you have accumulated quite a bit, squeeze the contents between two dry cloths and then put the cake away to cure. After a few weeks drying time the soap will be usable.
- Trim medical costs by refusing unnecessary duplication of tests. While it is perfectly all right if your gynecologist, your cardiologist, and your dermatologist all take your blood pressure, there is no reason for all three to take the same expensive lab tests if you have had the test recently. Tell them what tests you have had and the results and you will save quite a bit of money.
- Find out if the doctors in your area have established any sort of cooperative nighttime and weekend program. If so, these clinics generally charge less than you would pay at the emergency room of the hospital. These clinics deal primarily with emergency illnesses; for accident treatment you will still need to go to the hospital emergency room.
- Start a clothing exchange with your friends. Take advantage of the fact that children outgrow clothing long before it wears out. Assemble a group of mothers with children of varying ages and two or three times a year you can set up a clothing exchange in somebody's basement.
- Chemical air fresheners are expensive and can be dangerous for toddlers and house pets. Try making your own inex-

pensive air fresheners. An orange studded with whole cloves gives out a wonderful aroma. Crushed mint leaves make a room smell fresher, too. Other aromatic spices can be tied in tiny bundles inside colorful fabric scraps sewn to a ribbon. This can then be attached high enough on the wall to be out of the reach of children. (Some spices are poisonous in quantity.)

- Manufacturers throw away all sorts of materials and if you ask politely some will let you look through their dumpsters. *Ask first!* In this way I acquired several boxes of cotton fabric scraps for quilts.
- Add your own oil to your car if it needs it between oil changes. Buy some good quality oil when it is on sale, as it frequently is at discount department stores, and add it yourself when needed.
- When you need a new car, check to see if any of the rental firms in your area sell their surplus vehicles. You can buy a rental car with low mileage for considerably less than you would pay for the same vehicle on a dealer's lot. The automobile is usually the current year's model and is warranted. The price does not have to be dickered, and, since the salespeople apparently don't work on commission, there are none of the high pressure tactics that most people have come to associate with car buying.
- Make your own playground equipment for your children. Use a motorcycle tire to make a swing. If you have access to large tires, such as those used on tractor-trailer rigs, you can create sandboxes and toys for children to climb on. Railroad ties also make good sides for sandboxes.
- Give your children free entertainment. Have you ever seen a toddler who could resist plastic margarine tubs, metal pie plates, and wooden mixing spoons? Also popular are cardboard boxes. For older children chalk, bean bags, and homemade finger paint can fill a great many hours. Since preschoolers enjoy cutting pictures from magazines give them an old photo album with magnetic type pages to fill. When your child tires of a picture the cut-outs can be removed easily and another round of pictures inserted.

- Office supplies such as paper, envelopes, and other accessories are generally cheaper when purchased in bulk quantities at an office supply store. However, such things as pencils and inexpensive pens for school use are usually cheaper when purchased at discount department stores.
- Utilize the free cookbooks provided by many companies. You usually will find better recipes in company cookbooks than in any other publications because the companies want to entice you to buy their products. Even the cookbooks which are not free may be worth the small investment required. Look in current issues of women's magazines to determine what cookbook offers are available.
- If someone you know works for a data processing company ask if old print-out sheets are available. Many times these can be had free of charge and are just right for children to use as drawing paper.
- It takes no longer to cook a double batch of soup, stew, or spaghetti sauce than it does to cook enough for just one meal. By doubling up you can put one batch in the freezer to be used on a day when you don't have time to cook from scratch. The best kinds of convenience foods are those you make yourself.
- Do you like to use original artwork to decorate your home? If so, check with some local art students. Many are willing to sell their work for the price of the canvas and the paint. Also, many hobbyists will paint for you free of charge if you furnish the paint and canvas just because they enjoy painting.
- If you are having new kitchen countertops installed don't discard the cut-outs from the area where the sink is placed. These can be used for chopping boards, hot pads, or with the addition of four inexpensive wooden legs, become a weatherproof table to place beside your favorite lawn chair.
- Would you like to buy a house for one dollar? In some large cities this is possible. Because some old houses do not meet the codes for residential buldings these houses come into the possession of the city government. In order to encourage the revitalization of inner-city neighborhoods these houses are then sold for one dollar each. Most will require repairs which

will ultimately cost twenty thousand dollars or more, but for the do-it-yourselfer that is still a bargain. To qualify for these houses you must not own other property and you must agree to live in the house yourself.

- Rag dolls and soft toys can be stuffed with old nylons, lint from your clothes dryer, or sliced foam from a discarded mattress.
- If you wear knee-high stockings with your slacks or thigh-high stockings with your dresses, buy them in quantity. By having them all in the same color you can keep matching them up until all pairs are worn out.
- Before discarding old clothing remove the buttons, zippers, elastic, lace, and trims. All these things can be reused on a new garment. (Nylon zippers don't last as long as metal ones but they can frequently be reused if they have been well taken care of.)
- Are you looking for a bargain-priced house? If so, check the newspaper ads to determine if any VA or FHA repossessed houses are available in your area. These houses are offered at considerably lower prices than are houses being sold by individuals. An added advantage is that the houses are completely remodeled and in first-class shape.
- Organize a shopping carpool. If you want to visit an outlet store twenty-five or even fifty miles away, probably the cost of gasoline will be greater than the money you save on the goods you buy. However, if six people go, the bargain hunting becomes worthwhile and you gain a day's outing with your friends as well.
- Learn to enjoy free or inexpensive entertainment. The public library shows films. The recreation center teaches arts and crafts. The YMCA and YWCA offer various kinds of inexpensive classes. Shopping centers often set up displays or provide free shows such as programs featuring chorale groups or barbershop quartets or television personalities. Shopping malls feature such things as antique car shows, nostalgia items, art exhibits, needlework demonstrations, and rock and mineral shows. If the weekend finds you with no funds available for entertainment check to see what is going on at the local shopping malls.

- Learn everything you can. Libraries offer free courses in such things as photography and creative writing. Hobby shops offer everything from decoupage to quilting. Some bakeries offer low-cost cake decorating courses. Certain communities offer low-cost courses in such things as car repair, income tax preparation, and typing. If you live near a college check to see if they have a community program whereby non-credit courses are offered in things such as bookkeeping, accounting, music, art, or real estate. Everything you can learn to do provides one more opportunity for saving money.